Native Plant
GARDENING FOR
BIRDS, BEES & BUTTERFLIES

Northeast

Jaret C. Daniels

Adventure Publications
Cambridge, Minnesota

DEDICATION

To my wife, Stephanie, for her unconditional love and support. I am continuously grateful to have such an amazing person with whom to share my life.

ACKNOWLEDGMENTS

Thanks to my parents for their enduring encouragement of my interest in natural history and all things wild.

Cover and book design by Jonathan Norberg
Edited by Brett Ortler and Ritchey Halphen
Proofread by Dan Downing

All cover photos by Jaret C. Daniels unless otherwise noted.
(Front cover) birdhouse, **Dance60/shutterstock.com;** Cedar Waxwing, **Dennis W. Donohue /shutterstock.com;** Eastern Tiger Swallowtail, **Kevin Collison/shutterstock.com;** Yarrow, **Tatiana Belova/shutterstock.com;** Red Columbine, **Lynda H/shutterstock.com**
(Back cover) Common Prickly Ash (top bar), **Marinodenisenko/shutterstock.com;** American Copper butterfly, **Mirko Grauel/shutterstock.com;** Red Admiral butterfly, **Ian Grainger/shutterstock.com**

10 9 8 7 6 5 4 3 2

Native Plant Gardening for Birds, Bees & Butterflies: Northeast
Copyright © 2022 by Jaret C. Daniels
Published by Adventure Publications
An imprint of AdventureKEEN
310 Garfield Street South
Cambridge, Minnesota 55008
(800) 678-7006
www.adventurepublications.net
Printed in China
ISBN 978-1-64755-253-4 (pbk.); ISBN 978-1-64755-254-1 (ebook)

Table of Contents

Why You Should Plant a Garden. 4

   First Step: Inventory Your Yard 4

   Check Your Hardiness Zone. 4

   Space Considerations. 5

   Analyze Light Levels 5

   Take Slope & Elevation into Account. 5

   Analyzing Moisture Levels 6

   A Simple Soil-Texture Test 6

   Soil Testing. 6

   Interpreting Soil-Test Results 7

   Planning Ahead 7

   When to Plant 8

   Eliminating Existing Weeds 8

   The Seed Bank 9

   Nuisance Weeds. 10

   Improving the Soil 10

   Native Plants Matter. 10

   Plant Life Cycle 11

   Garden Design 11

   Plant Diversity 11

   Plant Selection at the Nursery 12

   Cultivars & Hybrids. 12

   Avoid Plants Treated with Pesticides. . . . 13

   Before You Plant, Stage Your Garden . . . 13

   Giving Plants a Good Start. 13

   Maintenance. 14

   Avoid Broad-Spectrum Insecticides 14

   Deadheading 14

   Staking Down Plants 14

   What to Do Before Winter 15

The Basics of Plant Anatomy 16

   Flowers 16

   Flower Terminology. 16

   Flower Clusters 17

   Leaf Types 17

   Leaf Attachments 17

Why Protect Pollinators?. 18

Meet the Pollinators 18

   Bees 18

   Butterflies. 19

   Moths. 19

   Beetles 20

   Flies 20

   Wasps 21

   Bee Mimics & Look-Alikes. 21

   Birds. 21

Native Plant Conservation 22

How to Use This Book 22

Northeast Plants at a Glance 23

Northeast Native Plants

Full Sun. 36

Full Sun to Partial Shade 120

Partial Shade to Full Shade. 216

Garden Plants for Butterflies 260

Garden Plants for Bees 262

Container Garden for Pollinators . . . 264

Bird Food & Nesting Plants 266

Hummingbird Plants. 267

Larval Host List. 268

Retail Sources of Northeast
   Native Seed & Plants. 272

Cooperative Extension Service 272

Native Plant Societies 272

Botanical Gardens & Arboretums. . . 272

Index 273

Photo Credits 278

About the Author 280

Why You Should Plant a Garden

Landscaping with native plants offers numerous benefits. First and foremost, it helps increase habitat and provides critical resources for wildlife. Studies have shown that including native plant species and increasing overall plant diversity help support a greater abundance and diversity of wildlife. Natives are adapted to the growing conditions, such as soil and climate, of the locations where they naturally occur. As a result, they tend to perform better than nonnative species once established, have fewer pest or disease problems, and require less water, fertilizer, and general maintenance—all of which can provide cost savings over time. Lastly, they add tremendous beauty to our landscapes and help provide increased opportunities for people to connect—or reconnect—with nature.

FIRST STEP: INVENTORY YOUR YARD

When you plant a garden, it's critical to select plants that will thrive on your property. This means considering a number of factors, such as light levels and soil conditions, but this isn't as complicated as it might seem at first. In fact, doing just a little homework ahead of time will improve your odds of growing healthy, beautiful plants—and attracting pollinators—dramatically.

CHECK YOUR HARDINESS ZONE

An easy first step is to check your hardiness zone. The USDA maintains the **Plant Hardiness Zone Map** (see below and planthardiness.ars.usda.gov), which can be used to help determine appropriate plants for your climate. It is divided into numbered 10°F increments (further divided into two zones

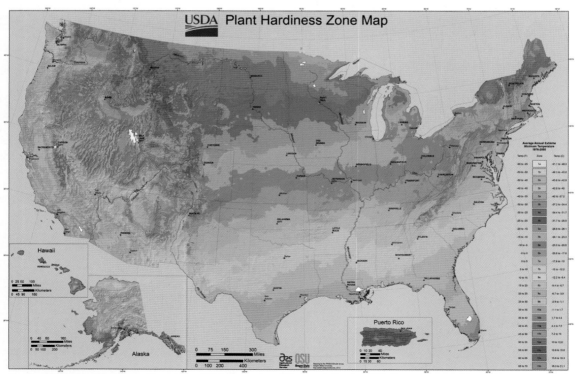

Credit: *USDA Plant Hardiness Zone Map,* 2012. Agricultural Research Service, U.S. Department of Agriculture. Accessed from planthardiness.ars.usda.gov.

per number), based on average annual extreme minimum winter temperature (the lowest temperature water reaches during an average year). So, for example, Hartford, Connecticut is Zone 6b, where the average extreme minimum temperature is -5 to 0°F, and about 200 miles north of there in Montpelier, Vermont, you'll encounter Zone 4b, where the average minimum temperature is -25 to -20°F.

In general, for best results, avoid plants that have a higher zone number than yours; they are more sensitive to cold temperatures and thus are unlikely to reliably survive over the long term. Note, however, that the Northeast is a large region—its climate varies tremendously north–south from Maine to New Jersey or Pennsylvania, and similarly from more-inland locations to coastal sites. This results in a USDA Hardiness Zone range of 3b–6b. So check carefully and pick plants specifically suited to the specific zone in which you live.

SPACE CONSIDERATIONS

Whether you have a sprawling meadow or just enough space for a container garden (see page 264), the first step when planning a garden is to establish how much room is available, as the overall garden area directly influences plant selection. Avoid the temptation to overcrowd the available space. Plants need room to grow, so think about how much space each plant will require once it matures, and be realistic. Use this guide and other resources to help determine each plant's height, overall form, and how much it spreads, and plan accordingly before putting it in the ground.

ANALYZE LIGHT LEVELS

Note how many hours of direct, unfiltered sunlight your proposed planting site receives in the summer. Plants labeled as **Full Sun** will thrive in sunny locations that receive at least 6 full hours of sunlight per day during the growing season. While such plants may still grow in locations that have less light, overall growth and flowering performance may be affected, often severely.

Plants characterized as **Partial Sun** or **Partial Shade** typically perform best with 4–6 hours of direct sunlight a day or dappled light for the duration of the day. They often thrive when exposed to early-day sun and may benefit from a bit less illumination during the hottest times of the afternoon.

Full Shade plants require fewer than 4 hours of direct sunlight. They often do quite well in locations with dappled shade and tend to prefer direct sun in the morning or the evening.

TAKE SLOPE & ELEVATION INTO ACCOUNT

When you're evaluating your yard's light levels, keep slope exposure in mind, and note the direction in which a planting site is angled. An area's slope affects the amount of light it receives. North-facing slopes, for example, receive less direct sunlight. With reduced heating, they are cooler, and the soil tends to remain moist for a longer period of time. Such sites also experience a longer period of frost. By contrast, south- and west-facing slopes receive ample sunlight. They tend to be hotter and have a somewhat longer growing season. With increased sun come increased transpiration and evaporation, making such sites drier; this means they often require increased irrigation to maintain adequate soil moisture. Plants that are more heat and drought tolerant are often ideal for such exposures. While the impact of slope on your plantings can be subtle, it is nonetheless worth considering, especially at higher latitudes (30–55 degrees North), where slope can have a greater impact on light levels.

On a similar note, site elevation is also worth considering. High points in the landscape, such as along the ridge of a berm, are often more exposed to wind. This tends to dry out soil more rapidly, batters plants, and produces harsher winter conditions. Such locations are challenging for tender or delicate species, which prefer more-protected sites. Instead, choose robust, drought-tolerant plants.

ANALYZING MOISTURE LEVELS

Likewise, site moisture is vital to evaluate. Is the site in question consistently wet, moist, average, or dry? In most cases, you can tell simply by visually inspecting the site on a regular basis. Wet sites, for example, can be characterized as being reliably soggy, whereas moist sites are simply damp. Site location and drainage may also be useful. Is the site adjacent to a stream, wetland, or depression? Does rainwater regularly flow into or collect in the site? Soil composition and texture, such as the proportion of clay, silt, or sand present, directly affect moisture retention and can be used to help assess site conditions.

Testing soil texture

A SIMPLE SOIL-TEXTURE TEST

If you're not sure, conduct a quick soil-texture test. To do so, dig down about 6–8 inches with a shovel or trowel, and grab a handful of soil. First, rub a small amount through your fingers. How does it feel? Sandy soil is a bit coarse and feels somewhat gritty, whereas clay tends to feel a little sticky. Next, grab another handful. Moisten it slightly, squeeze it into a ball, and then open your hand. Sandy soil tends to fall apart almost immediately. Loamy soil, which contains a mix of sand and clay, generally holds its shape but crumbles somewhat when prodded. Clay soil, by contrast, remains firmly together in a ball and resists breaking apart when pressure is applied.

SOIL TESTING

While it's not a necessity when planting a garden, it's often useful to get your soil tested. As soil properties directly affect plant growth and performance, knowing your soil's pH level—how acidic or alkaline it is—can, along with its nutrient levels, provide valuable insight, helping you select plants that are best suited for your specific conditions. Soil testing also helps you determine the best way to augment the existing soil and how to select the most efficient fertilizers if you opt to fertilize.

A pH test kit

Better yet, soil testing is simple and inexpensive. Most basic soil tests, which analyze pH, organic matter, and the levels of several basic essential nutrients, cost about $20 and often less. They're available at many home improvement stores, garden centers, and online. Local county extension offices also often test soil; for more information, see "Cooperative Extension Service," page 272.

When testing soil, be sure to test multiple areas, as soil conditions may vary depending on location and nearby trees or vegetation. If you really want to know everything about your soil, there are tests that go far beyond the basics, including tests for salt levels, trace elements, and even lead contamination.

INTERPRETING SOIL-TEST RESULTS

The chart below shows a number of common soil nutrients and micronutrients. When you get your soil tested, you'll receive a report indicating how acidic your soil is and the range of nutrients (and in some cases, micronutrients) present in your soil. You can then use this information when planning your garden and preparing any future soil amendments.

Soil pH & Nutrient Availability

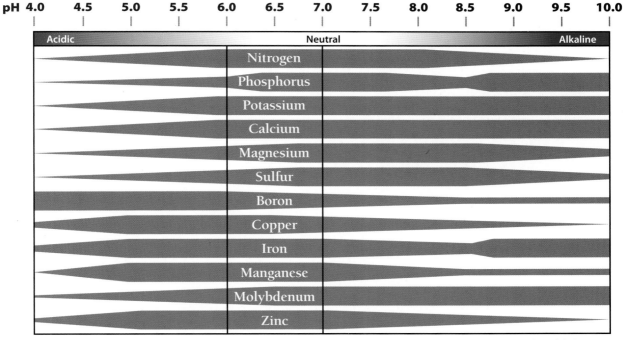

Optimum soil availability

PLANNING AHEAD

In all cases, a little planning will produce better results: Your plants will perform better, your landscape will look more attractive, and most importantly, you (and the pollinators) will be happier. The cardinal rule is simple: pick the right plant for the location. For example, avoid forcing a sun-loving species into a shady spot. Instead, tailor your design and plant choices to your landscape's conditions. This is the only sure recipe for success.

WHEN TO PLANT

There is no hard-and-fast rule regarding the best time to plant. Most gardeners are generally accustomed to planting in spring, once the growing season begins. This allows new plants ample time to get established, grow, and add beauty to the landscape. It also gives them a head start before the summer heat arrives, which can add to plant stress and necessitate more frequent irrigation. Planting during hot and dry conditions requires extra care and attention for best results, so keep this in mind if adding plants to your landscape during the summer months or during periods of abnormal heat or drought.

Fall planting is often ideal. The weather is often more predictable than in spring and the heat less intense compared with the peak of summer. The resulting milder, more-stable conditions reduce plant stress. Soil temperatures are also quite warm, which helps stimulate root growth. Moreover, the germination of many weeds tends to wind down later in the season, which typically means less competition for the new plantings. Collectively, these conditions lead to increased plant growth and more rapid overall establishment. For maximum success, however, plan to get all plants in the ground with at least one month of the growing season remaining. This ensures that they have time to grow before chances of frost increase. Fall is also an ideal time to divide perennials if needed.

Removing weeds by hand is effective but also labor-intensive.

ELIMINATING EXISTING WEEDS

Weeds are certainly among the biggest challenges and frustrations in the garden. Unfortunately, there is no silver bullet for controlling them. Good site preparation before you plant can make quite a difference, however. It can substantially minimize future weed pressure, and in turn it provides plants with better growing conditions. As with all other aspects of landscaping, it is useful to develop a detailed and realistic site-preparation plan ahead of time.

In general, there are three main weed issues to consider. The first is obvious: eliminating existing weeds. Depending on the size of your site and the number of weeds, this can be done either by simple hand removal or by weed torching, tilling, or applying a nonselective herbicide such as glyphosate directly to the weed foliage. If using a herbicide, be sure to carefully follow all the label instructions—*to the letter*—regarding application and safety. For larger sites, or sites with an increased weed load, herbicide application is typically the most labor- and cost-effective method. In this case, it is useful to mow the site, wait a few weeks until the weeds start to regrow, and then apply herbicide. A final mow (after a waiting period for the herbicide to take effect; check the label) will then clear away most of the dead weed debris. In some cases, more than one cycle of herbicide application and mowing, spaced out about two to four weeks apart, may be necessary to get the best results. Note that for sites infested with weedy grasses, additional measures may be needed to produce effective control. When the weeds are removed, be sure to review the herbicide label for any potential residual effects that may negatively affect subsequent seeding or planting.

THE SEED BANK

The second weed-related issue to consider is the seed bank, or weed seeds present in the soil that can germinate later, presenting a problem. If you want to avoid chemicals, soil solarization is one particularly useful strategy to try in warmer portions of the region. This simple method can be readily applied to both large or small areas. It involves covering existing soil with clear plastic and taking advantage of sunlight to heat the soil to a temperature sufficient to kill weeds, weed seeds, and potentially a range of soil pests and pathogens.

Soil solarization in progress

For best results, conduct soil solarization during the warmest months of the year. Start by clearing the area of all plants and associated debris; this ensures that the plastic can lie directly on the surface of the soil without forming large air pockets. Next, water the soil thoroughly. Moisture is a good conductor of heat and helps increase its penetration into the soil. Cover the area with clear plastic sheeting, which is relatively inexpensive and available at home improvement stores and garden centers. It is useful to use a somewhat thicker (higher-mil) product, usually 1.5 mil or greater, as it will help resist tears and punctures. Once the area is fully covered, bury the ends in soil or otherwise weigh them down with soil, bricks, lumber, or other material. This ensures that the plastic is sufficiently anchored and removes any air gaps, so that it can easily trap heat. To maximize effectiveness, it is generally recommended to leave the soil covered for four to eight weeks.

Soil-applied herbicides are another option to combat the weed seed bank. These are applied to the soil after target plants have been established, and they create a barrier that kills weeds shortly after they germinate. They can provide effective residual control of various common broadleaf weeds and some annual weedy grasses for several weeks. Application may need to be repeated several times during the growing season for longer prevention. It is important to understand that no herbicide provides complete control, and some products may injure existing plants or turf. As with other chemicals, always thoroughly read the label before use, and carefully follow the manufacturer's safety and application instructions.

NUISANCE WEEDS

The last main weed issue to address is nuisance weed control after plant establishment. Well-executed site preparation and planning can greatly reduce—but never completely eliminate—nuisance weeds. Beyond often being unattractive, weeds compete with your plants for resources, including light, water, and nutrients. Minor spot-weeding can often easily be done by hand or with the use of a weed torch. This should be done regularly for best control. Mulching is often one of the best ways to suppress nuisance weeds and significantly reduces the need for spot control, which can be time-consuming and inconvenient. Mulch also helps retain soil moisture and maintain a more consistent soil temperature, which can lessen plant stress, enhance plant growth, and reduce how much you need to water. Mulch can beautify an area by providing a neat and manicured look. Many natural mulches even help add organic material to the soil over time as they decompose.

Compost is a popular soil amendment.

IMPROVING THE SOIL

Many soils require improvement to enhance their overall quality and structure. Organic matter such as compost, animal manure, straw, shredded wood chips, fallen leaves, and peat are common choices. These help improve fertility, water and nutrient retention, aeration, permeability, and other soil properties, which in turn promote healthy plant growth. Most organic amendments are easy to obtain. Compost, for example, is relatively simple to make yourself, or you can buy it from a local garden center. (Be aware that some organic matter, such as manure, may contain weed seeds.) Beyond organic matter, additional amendments such as sand, gravel, vermiculite, or perlite can also be used to help improve various soil properties. You can even use various amendments to tweak the soil pH or address key mineral or other nutrient deficiencies. Before doing so, consult your soil-test results (see page 6) and use them as a guide. You may also wish to get advice from a nursery professional or local extension agent.

NATIVE PLANTS MATTER

Studies have shown that including native plant species and increasing the overall plant diversity in your garden helps promote species diversity. Connecting these wildlife-friendly landscapes into a wider network—think of it as a pollinator trail of sorts—helps native pollinators and birds more easily and safely move from one place to another, maintains healthier wildlife populations and habitats, and improves or creates more opportunities for people to connect or reconnect with nature. By doing so, we can establish healthier and more-sustainable spaces for wildlife and humans alike.

PLANT LIFE CYCLE

Plants are generally characterized by their life cycle. While most woody plants are relatively long-lived, herbaceous species can be divided into three main categories: *annuals, perennials,* and *biennials.* Annuals complete their entire life cycle from initial germination to seeding in a single growing season. Only the seed, but not the plant, survives. Such species need to be planted anew each year or will germinate from seed dispersed by previous years' plants. Perennials, by contrast, survive and continue to grow for several years, with many surviving for much longer. Lastly, biennials take two years to complete development. The first year is one of root, stem, and leaf growth, while flowering and seed production are completed in the second full season. The original plant does not return for a third year of growth.

Black-Eyed Susan

GARDEN DESIGN

Before you begin putting plants in the ground, it is helpful to make a basic plan or design sketch. Review the requirements and key features of each plant, such as light, moisture, and soil preferences, mature size and spread, bloom time, flower color, leaf color, and fall color. Such information will help guide plant placement and your overall landscape design. Then group plants with similar requirements together: place the tallest plants in the back of the bed and shorter plants in the foreground, but keep light levels and sun direction in mind.

The total planting area available and its configuration will influence plant selection and quantity. For example, perennial borders tend to be more-narrow, linear spaces accessed from only one side. By comparison, cottage gardens can be more expansive and creatively designed. It is also often beneficial to group multiple plants of the same species together. Odd numbers of plant groupings are typically most visually pleasing, as this provides waves or blocks of color and texture in the landscape. For larval host plants, it also provides increased food resources for hungry larvae.

PLANT DIVERSITY

In general, increased plant diversity helps support a greater abundance and diversity of wildlife. If this is your goal, design your landscape accordingly. Pick plants that offer a wide range of quality resources of nectar, pollen, seed, fruit, and larval food. Be sure to include species that offer resources throughout the growing season, not just at one particular time period. This is particularly important for pollinating insects. Additionally, choose blooming plants that display a variety of flower color, size, and shape. For example, plants with long, tubular blossoms may be most accessible and attractive to hummingbirds but not to smaller bees or butterflies. Lastly, pick plants that vary in height and form. This will provide needed structure in the landscape that in turn offers shelter, cover, nesting sites, perches, forage, or needed shade.

PLANT SELECTION AT THE NURSERY

Choosing plants for your landscape can be fun and highly rewarding. Nonetheless, some general best practices will help ensure the best possible outcome. Consult your yard inventory, and remember to select plants that match the conditions of your property and the specific site in question. If you purchase plants from a home or garden center, local nursery, or plant sale, take time to carefully inspect each one. When buying plants, be choosy. Examine all parts of the plant. Avoid plants with damaged stems, branches, or roots, yellowing or wilted leaves, or that otherwise have an overall unhealthy appearance. If you have doubts, it's probably good to stick with your instincts. Remember, you are making an investment in your property, so opt for the cream of the crop, such as plants with lush, robust, healthy foliage and a symmetrical form overall. These will likely perform best and make your landscape look its best.

Choose plants for your garden with care.

When purchasing native plants or seed, especially by mail, it is important to select varieties that are native to your region and locality. This seed stock is adapted to the environmental conditions of your region, so the resulting plants will typically perform much better. For example, stock from Colorado or North Carolina probably will not do as well in New York or the rest of the Northeast, owing to differences in soil and climate. Purchasing local and regional ecotypes additionally helps safeguard the genetic integrity of native plants in your area.

CULTIVARS & HYBRIDS

The topic of cultivars and hybrids is often highly contentious. Cultivars of native species, often referred to as "nativars," represent plants that have been specifically bred to select for a specific, desirable characteristic. This might include traits such as height, form, leaf color, or flower size or color. The resulting cultivars are often more flashy than their true native counterparts or offer additional options for gardeners that can enhance their appeal and broad horticultural marketability. Commercial cultivars of many common natives, such as *Gaillardia, Liatris, Echinacea, Coreopsis,* and *Symphyotrichum,* to name but a few, are readily available. Hybrids are reproductive crosses between two different but often closely related species with the goal of combining the best features of both. Many cultivars are hybrids.

Be aware that there are potential drawbacks to some cultivars and hybrids, and many are often misleadingly sold as natives. Double- or triple-flowered varieties, for example, while attractive, often make it difficult for pollinators to access nectar and pollen. Many others are sterile and do not produce viable seeds or fruit. Others may lack nectar altogether or provide floral rewards with reduced nutritional benefits. These have limited value and attractiveness to landscapes designed to benefit birds, pollinators, and other wildlife. When in doubt, purchase plants from nurseries specializing in natives, or contact your local native plant society, botanical garden, arboretum, or extension office for recommendations on suppliers.

AVOID PLANTS TREATED WITH PESTICIDES

Special care should be taken when purchasing plants that you hope will serve as larval hosts for caterpillars or as nectar plants for butterflies and other pollinating insects. Many plants sold at retailers, particularly those at larger garden centers, are often treated with pesticides to help control insect pests and resulting plant damage. While all pesticides pose a danger to insects, systemic pesticides, such as neonicotinoids, are among the most worrisome. Systemic pesticides are chemicals that are soluble in water and can be readily absorbed by a plant. They are relatively long-lasting to provide extended protection against sap- and leaf-feeding insects. Unfortunately, treated plants can

Check for this sign at your local garden center.

be deadly to butterfly larvae, and there is evidence that some products contaminate flower pollen and nectar, resulting in potential harm to bees and other insect pollinators. Therefore, it is critical to always ascertain if the plants you're buying have been treated. Avoid treated plants, and if you're not sure about a plant, find a different supplier. Unfortunately, there is no quick-and-easy test.

BEFORE YOU PLANT, STAGE YOUR GARDEN

When you're planning a garden, don't crowd plants. It's easy to forget that they will grow and increase in size, often dramatically, as they mature, so plan, and plant, accordingly. When your draft plan is finalized and you've acquired your plants and seeds, place all plants in their specific locations in the landscape for review. Look at the site from multiple angles, and adjust if needed. When happy, finish by putting all plants in the ground.

GIVING PLANTS A GOOD START

New plants perform their best with help right from the beginning. This includes initial planting. Start by digging a hole at least twice as wide as the root ball and just as deep. Next, gently remove the plant from its pot. Loosen the root ball by massaging the roots, separating them somewhat with your fingers, and place it in the hole. For bare-root plants, carefully spread out the roots when planting. Avoid placing the plant deeper than the original level in the pot, and do not place horticultural oil (a pesticide) on top of the root ball. Doing so can threaten the long-term health and performance of the plant. Once the root ball is in the hole, backfill with soil about half or three-quarters of the way upward, then gently tamp down the soil, and water. This will help the soil settle and remove any air pockets. Then fill the remainder of the hole with soil, and firmly compress it. Finally, water new plants regularly for at least the first three weeks. Following these steps will help ensure that your new plants have a strong start and are ready to perform.

MAINTENANCE

Most perennial plants, shrubs, and trees will thrive for years if well cared for. Do your homework to better understand the basic long-term needs of your plants, including watering, fertilization, pest and disease control, pruning, and winter care. Remember that a little basic planning and maintenance can make a huge difference. The goal is to have happy, healthy, and productive plants. A good example is pest control. While plant pests can be a nuisance, all big issues start out small. By regularly examining your plants, you can easily discover pests before they become a larger problem. Once found, always address pest problems at a local level. Simply removing insect pests by pruning off the affected part of the plant or by spraying them with a strong jet of water can help significantly. Insecticidal soaps and horticultural oils can be good options, but they often have negative impacts on the environment and nontarget species.

Aphids and other insects may be annoying, but you should nonetheless avoid broad-spectrum insecticides.

AVOID BROAD-SPECTRUM INSECTICIDES

Broad-spectrum insecticides are designed to kill a wide range of insects and can harm many of the beneficial species that you wish to attract. If you must use these toxic chemicals, always treat pest problems as locally as possible, and never spray or apply pesticides to your entire garden or landscape. Consult your local nursery professional or extension agent to help identify specific plant pest or disease issues and determine a viable solution. These experts can additionally help provide recommendations for effective pruning and fertilizing.

DEADHEADING

Many flowering perennials benefit from removing spent blossoms, or deadheading. This can help give plants a more manicured appearance and promote repeated blooming, which can in turn extend the flowering time of many species and provide added floral resources for pollinating insects. With that said, deadheading will prevent seeds or fruit from developing, and such food resources are also beneficial for many forms of wildlife, such as songbirds. So just how much to deadhead is something of a balancing act.

STAKING DOWN PLANTS

Some tall perennials or even newly planted trees may need to be staked. This can provide additional support, help prevent them from leaning or flopping over, and keep weaker upright stems or flowering stalks from bending or possibly breaking. Supports can also help elevate vines or rambling plants in the landscape, thereby enhancing their visual interest, appearance, and even performance.

WHAT TO DO BEFORE WINTER

As cold weather approaches, there is often some debate about how to prepare your landscape—whether or not you should cut back the dead foliage on perennials or leave it standing. In general, this is more of an aesthetic issue than one of essential plant care. With landscapes designed for wildlife in mind, it is best to leave the dead foliage, stems, and flower heads in place. Not only do the remains of many flowering perennials and grasses provide highly attractive visual interest during the drab winter months, but various species also provide

Dead foliage helps out wildlife.

valuable food or shelter to songbirds and other wildlife. The exception is particularly tender perennials, such as those at the margin of their normal hardiness zone—such plants often require a little extra care to help them survive winter temperatures. Start by cutting off the dead vegetation just a few inches above the soil surface. Leaving a few inches of vegetation will help you keep track of the plant in your landscape and prevent any potential damage to the roots. Next, cover the plant with several inches of mulch. This will help it conserve moisture and will insulate the soil, protecting it. Desiccation and freezing temperatures can injure or kill more-tender plants.

Eastern Tiger Swallowtail Butterfly on a Purple Coneflower

The Basics of Plant Anatomy

Plants are complex living things. Their typical body plan consists of detailed structures, including leaves, stems, and roots, along with reproductive parts that include flowers, fruits, and seeds. Flowers represent the sexual reproductive organs of a plant. The male organs are called *stamens;* each stamen includes a pollen-bearing *anther* atop an elongated *filament.* The *pistil* represents the female organ. It includes a

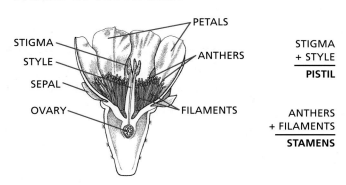

PARTS OF A FLOWER

STIGMA
STYLE
SEPAL
OVARY
PETALS
ANTHERS
FILAMENTS

STIGMA + STYLE
PISTIL

ANTHERS + FILAMENTS
STAMENS

stigma, which receives and holds pollen and has a sticky surface. The majority of flowering plants that gardeners are familiar with are *bisexual* (or *perfect,* in horticultural parlance), meaning they have flowers with both male and female elements. Other plants bear *unisexual* (or *imperfect*) flowers: *monoecious* plants have both male and female flowers on the same plant; in contrast, *dioecious* plants bear male and female blooms on separate individual plants. Some examples of dioecious plants include holly (*Ilex* spp.), Pussy Willow (*Salix discolor*), and Staghorn Sumac (*Rhus typhina*).

FLOWERS

Flowers are arguably the showiest parts of a plant. In most cases, conspicuous and colorful petals surround the reproductive parts. They help publicize the availability of floral rewards, such as pollen and nectar, to an array of pollinating organisms. All the petals of a flower are collectively called the *corolla.* *Sepals* occur below the corolla. Like petals, they are modified leaves; frequently green in color and relatively small, they help protect the developing flower bud and support the corolla when in bloom. This outermost whorl of flower components is called the *calyx.* In some cases, however, sepals may be large and brightly colored. This typically occurs in flowering plant species that lack petals.

FLOWER TERMINOLOGY

Botanically speaking, there are many types of flowers, but they can be simplified into five basic types. *Regular flowers* have a round shape, with three or more petals, and they lack a disklike center. *Irregular flowers* are not round but uniquely shaped, with fused petals. *Bell flowers* hang down with fused petals. *Tube flowers* are longer and narrower than bell flowers and point upwards. *Composite flowers* (technically a flower cluster) are usually round, compact clusters of tiny flowers that look like they are one larger bloom.

Regular   **Irregular**   **Bell**   **Tube**   **Composite**

FLOWER CLUSTERS

The grouping of numerous flowers on a stem is called an *inflorescence,* or flower cluster. There are three main kinds of flower clusters, and they are based on shape: *flat, round,* or *spike.*

Flat   **Round**   **Spike**

LEAF TYPES

There are two main kinds of leaves: *simple* and *compound.* Simple leaves are leaves that are in one piece; the leaf is not divided into smaller leaflets. The leaf can have teeth or be smooth along the edges. It may have lobes and indentations that give the leaf its unique shape. Compound leaves have two or more distinct small leaves, or leaflets, arising from a single stalk. They can be broadly categorized as *regular compound, twice compound,* or *palmate.* Twice compound leaves are those with many distinct leaflets that arise from a secondary leaf stalk. Palmate compound leaves have three or more leaflets arising from a common central point.

Simple   **Compound**   **Twice Compound**   **Palmate**

LEAF ATTACHMENTS

Leaves attach to the stem in a number of different ways: *alternately, oppositely,* in a *whorl, perfoliately, clasping,* or *basally.* Sometimes a plant can have two different types of attachments. This is most often seen in the combination of basal leaves and leaves that attach to the main stem. For most plants, there is only one type of leaf attachment.

Alternate leaves attach to the stem in an alternating pattern, while opposite leaves attach to the stem directly opposite from one another. Whorled leaves have three or more leaves that attach around the stem at the same point. Perfoliate leaves are stalkless and have a leaf base that completely surrounds the main stem. Clasping leaves have no stalk, and the base of the leaf only partially surrounds the main stem. Basal leaves originate at the base of the plant, near the ground, and are usually grouped in a rosette.

Alternate   **Opposite**   **Whorled**   **Perfoliate**   **Clasping**   **Basal**

Why Protect Pollinators?

Pollination is essential. Globally, more than 85 percent of all flowering plant species rely on or benefit from animals, primarily insects, for pollination. These many organisms move pollen from one blossom to another, enabling the plants to produce fruit, seeds, and the next generation of flowering plants. Without pollinators, it would be impossible to maintain productive, diverse natural plant communities and ensure the functionality of our agricultural lands. Alarmingly, many recent studies indicate that insect pollinator populations are declining in many regions, including the United States and Europe. Some of the hardest-hit groups include bees, moths, and butterflies, important pollinators for many wild and cultivated plants, including various specialty crops. As habitat loss and degradation are the primary drivers of these declines, rebuilding wildlife-friendly landscapes is more important than ever.

That's where you come in. Gardening for wildlife is a fun and rewarding endeavor. Now more than ever, the choices we make in our own landscapes matter. While such spaces can never replace pristine natural environments, they can provide pollinators and birds with important food, nesting, and shelter resources and help reduce the many impacts of habitat fragmentation and urbanization. A growing body of research supports the wildlife-conservation benefit of these nontraditional lands. Private yards and home gardens collectively compose the largest percentage of green space in most urban areas. Additionally, as the majority of Americans now live in cities and their surrounding suburbs, yards and gardens offer tremendous potential for each of us to make a difference.

Meet the Pollinators

While bees, especially the Western Honeybee (*Apis mellifera*, also known as the European Honeybee), get most of the attention, when it comes to pollination, many other insects regularly visit flowers and serve as pollinators. The most common groups include butterflies, moths, beetles, flies, and wasps.

BEES

North America boasts some 4,000 different bee species, with several hundred species occurring in the Northeast. Maine has some 270 species, with New York boasting over 400 species. With the exception of the nonnative Western Honeybee and a few other introduced species, the rest are native, and the majority of bees actually lead solitary lifestyles. They also display a wide range of sizes, colors, and behaviors, making them fascinating and attractive garden visitors. Collectively, bees are arguably

the most effective and efficient insect pollinators. Beyond visiting flowers for nectar, they also actively collect pollen. These raw materials represent the primary food resources for adult bees and their developing young. In other words, they are highly motivated to make many flower visits and transport pollen, the components necessary for successful pollination. In addition, bees actively forage for floral resources in and around the landscape in which they nest. The majority of bees are generalists; like hungry patrons visiting a buffet, they visit a broad array of different flowers, preferring plants with large amounts of high-quality resources when available.

1. Western Honeybee (*Apis mellifera*) **2.** Eastern Bumblebee (*Bombus impatiens*) **3.** Eastern Carpenter Bee (*Xylocopa virginica*) **4.** Leaf-cutter bee (*Megachile* spp.) **5.** Sweat bee (*Agapostemon* spp., *Halictus* spp.) **6.** Long-horned bee (*Melissodes* spp.)

BUTTERFLIES

Butterflies are among the most recognizable and charismatic insects. Their tremendous appeal makes them ideal "gateway bugs" to help people connect with the natural world. Not surprisingly, butterfly gardening and butterfly watching are soaring in popularity nationwide. While the greatest diversity of butterflies occurs in tropical regions of the world, North America is home to around 800 different species, with more than 150 species found in the Northeast.

All adult butterflies feed on liquids. Most species in our area consume sugar-rich nectar; this potent energy source helps power their flight and virtually all other activities. This is why butterflies are highly attracted to colorful blooming flowers. With the exception of a few tropical butterflies that actively collect and feed on pollen, all other species visit flowers to sip nectar. In the process of feeding, they often brush against the flowers' anthers and inadvertently pick up pollen on their head, body, or wings, making them important pollinators.

1. Black Swallowtail (*Papilio polyxenes*) **2.** Cloudless Sulphur (*Phoebis sennae*) **3.** Eastern Tailed-Blue (*Everes comyntas*) **4.** Viceroy (*Limenitis archippus*) **5.** Common Wood Nymph (*Cercyonis pegala*) **6.** Hobomok Skipper (*Poanes hobomok*)

MOTHS

Compared with butterflies, moths are much more diverse. There are over 150 butterfly species in the Northeast, but there are more than 2,750 species of moths. Despite this diversity, moths tend to be poorly studied and are often overlooked. As a result, relatively little is known about how much this primarily nocturnal group contributes to plant pollination. Nonetheless, recent research suggests that moths play a particularly important role as pollinators, including as pollinators of specialty agricultural crops, augmenting the work of bees and other flower-visiting insects. Moths may also help improve the genetic diversity of plants because they transport pollen over greater distances than bees. Additional studies will almost certainly reveal that moths play a critical role as pollinators.

1. White-Lined Sphinx Moth (*Hyles lineata*) **2.** Virginia Ctenucha Moth (*Ctenucha virginica*) **3.** Garden Tiger Moth (*Arctia caja*) **4.** Eight-Spotted Forester (*Alypia octomaculata*) **5.** Snowberry Clearwing Moth (*Hemaris diffinis*) **3.** Ailanthus Webworm Moth (*Atteva aurea*)

BEETLES

Beetles represent the largest and most diverse order of insects. In North America alone, there are approximately 28,000 species, and that's just a mere 7 percent of the global total. Due to their tremendous numbers alone, beetles represent the largest group of pollinating animals, but not all beetles visit flowers. Those that do, visit in search of food, typically feeding on pollen, but they may also munch away on various flower parts and, less often, nectar. As beetles are typically somewhat clumsy, bulky insects, they need to physically land on and crawl across blossoms to feed, and in the process they frequently pick up pollen grains. They are most often encountered on larger open flowers or flowers with sizable clusters. This wonderful group of insects boasts a truly dizzying array of individual sizes, colors, and shapes, making observation fun and highly rewarding.

1. Goldenrod Soldier Beetle (*Chauliognathus pensylvanicus*) **2.** Locust Borer (*Megacyllene robiniae*) **3.** Banded Net-Winged Beetle (*Calopteron reticulatum*) **4.** Tumbling Flower Beetles (*Mordella* spp.) **5.** Firefly (*Photinus* spp.) **6.** Dark Flower Scarab Beetle (*Euphoria sepulcralis*)

FLIES

With approximately 17,000 species found in North America, flies are another large and highly diverse group of insects, and a great many of them—even mosquitoes—frequent flowers. They typically feed on sugar-rich nectar and occasionally pollen. Even though they have something of a negative reputation, flies are prolific and important pollinators, visiting a wide range of flowering plants, including many important crops, such as cherries, apples, pears, strawberries, and raspberries, among others. In addition, the larvae of many species play other key roles in the environment, including as predators that provide natural pest control or as decomposers, helping to break down dead plant and animal material. Some fly groups, such as hoverflies (or flower flies), have a particularly strong predilection for flowers, and many species are highly convincing bee or wasp mimics.

1. Hoverfly (Syrphidae family) **2.** Flesh Fly (Sarcophagidae family) **3.** Green Bottle Fly (*Lucilia sericata*) **4.** Mosquito (Culicidae family) **5.** Crane Fly (Tipulidae family) **6.** Swift Feather-Legged Fly (*Trichopoda pennipes*)

WASPS

Together with bees and ants, wasps belong to the order Hymenoptera, the third-largest group of insects. Despite often being feared, the vast majority of wasps are actually solitary and nonaggressive, and they don't pose a stinging hazard. By contrast, social wasps, such as yellow jackets, paper wasps, and hornets, can deliver a painful sting and will actively defend their nests if disturbed or threatened. Collectively, wasps are highly beneficial insects. Many are important pollinators that frequent a wide range of flowering plants. The adults are equally valuable predators or parasites of a wide range of insects, including many pest species. Taken as a whole, wasps are far more beneficial to the ecosystem—and to us—than we give them credit for.

1. Northern Paper Wasp (*Polistes fuscatus*) **2.** Bald-Faced Hornet (*Dolichovespula maculata*) **3.** Blue Mud Dauber (*Chalybion californicum*) **4.** Four-Banded Stink Bug Hunter Wasp (*Bicyrtes quadrifasciatus*) **5.** Common Thread-Waisted Wasp (*Ammophila procera*) **6.** Two-Spotted Scoliid Wasp (*Scolia dubia*)

BEE MIMICS & LOOK-ALIKES

Looks can be deceiving: a range of flower-visiting insects mimics bees or wasps, displaying superficially similar yellow-and-black color patterns to scare off would-be predators. While a great many of these look-alikes are flies, some day-flying moths and even a scarab beetle or two get in on the act. Thus, it is important not to jump to quick conclusions when you spot a brightly colored insect. It takes careful observation to recognize these superb disguises.

1. Maize Calligrapher (*Toxomerus politus*) **2.** Bee fly (Bombyliidae family) **3.** Thysbe Hummingbird Moth (*Hemaris thysbe*) **4.** Hoverfly (*Syrphidae* family) **5.** Wasp Mimic Moth (*Vitacea polistiformis*) **6.** Delta Flower Scarab (*Trigonopeltastes delta*)

BIRDS

Birds are popular and welcomed garden visitors. Beyond their broad appeal, birds provide a range of valuable services to the landscape. Ruby-Throated Hummingbirds are colorful and entertaining flower visitors that help pollinate numerous plant species. A great many birds, such as bluebirds, wrens, woodpeckers, swallows, and crows, also feed on insects. This is especially true during breeding season, when insects make up the majority of the high-protein diet adult birds feed to their young. In the process, they provide natural pest control and help keep plant-feeding insect populations in check. Still others help manage weeds by consuming large quantities of seed from aggressive or otherwise undesirable plants.

Fruit-feeding birds play a key role in seed dispersal. In fact, hundreds of plant species rely on our feathered friends for this valuable service. In doing so, birds help maintain healthy and diverse native plant populations.

Native Plant Conservation

Native plant populations are critical components of the ecosystem, so please don't collect native plants or seeds from the wild. This can harm existing habitat, threaten local native plant populations, and adversely affect pollinators and other wildlife that rely on them for food. Additionally, in many instances, collecting native plants from the wild may be illegal. Instead, always purchase or acquire native plants from a reputable grower or source (see page 272 for recommendations).

How to Use This Book

All of the plants in this book are native plants, and they are organized by light requirements, with sections for **Full Sun, Full Sun to Partial Shade,** and **Partial Shade to Full Shade.** Each plant account includes information on the plant's size and growth pattern, hardiness zone, its bloom period, and what it attracts, as well as specific notes about the plant. When planning your garden, you can either find plants that strike your fancy by paging through the book, or you can consult the butterfly- and bee-specific garden plans on pages 260–264. If you're looking to attract a specific type of butterfly or caterpillar, see pages 268–271 for a list of larval hosts; also see page 267 for a list of plants that attract hummingbirds. For a list of plants that provide Bird Food & Nesting Sites see page 266. And once you have your garden planned out, turn to page 272 for a list of some of the retail suppliers of native plants in the Northeast.

Northeast Plants at a Glance

The Northeast covers a large area, spanning from Maine south to the Atlantic coast of New Jersey and west through New York and Pennsylvania to the shores of Lake Erie. With such a wide geographic range to consider, choosing plants for your garden can seem a bit overwhelming. That's why we've created the following at-a-glance resource to help you decide what to plant.

It includes everything from hardiness zone, light level, and soil preference to bloom period and whether the plant attracts butterflies, bees, or birds.

Note: Browsing deer can cause damage to plants. While such feeding may simply be a nuisance, it can at times be quite destructive to a garden or landscape. Few plants are 100 percent deer-proof, especially if deer populations are large or available food resources are limited. Nonetheless, several species are considered moderately or highly resistant to deer, and they are indicated in the table on the following pages.

A vibrant wildflower garden

Northeast Plants at a Glance

	COMMON NAME	SCIENTIFIC NAME	LIGHT LEVEL	NORTHEAST HARDINESS ZONE
FULL SUN				
	Big Bluestem pg. 39	*Andropogon gerardii*	full sun	4a–7b
	Black-Eyed Susan pg. 41	*Rudbeckia hirta*	full sun	3a–7b
	Blue Flag Iris pg. 43	*Iris virginica*	full sun	4a–7b
	Blue Vervain pg. 45	*Verbena hastata*	full sun	3a–7b
	Butterflyweed pg. 47	*Asclepias tuberosa*	full sun	3a–7b
	Common Milkweed pg. 49	*Asclepias syriaca*	full sun	3a–7b
	Common Ninebark pg. 51	*Physocarpus opulifolius*	full sun	2a–7b
	Common Sneezeweed pg. 53	*Helenium autumnale*	full sun	3a–7b
	Common Yarrow pg. 55	*Achillea millefolium*	full sun	3a–7b
	Culver's Root pg. 57	*Veronicastrum virginicum*	full sun	3a–7b
	Cup Plant pg. 59	*Silphium perfoliatum*	full sun	3a–7b
	Dense Blazing Star pg. 61	*Liatris spicata*	full sun	3a–7b
	Devil's Bite pg. 63	*Liatris scariosa*	full sun	3a–7b
	False Aster pg. 65	*Boltonia asteroides*	full sun	3a–7b
	Field Thistle pg. 67	*Cirsium discolor*	full sun	3a–7b
	Garden Phlox pg. 69	*Phlox paniculata*	full sun	4a–7b
	Hairy Lespedeza pg. 71	*Lespedeza hirta*	full sun	4b–7b
	Hoary Vervain pg. 73	*Verbena stricta*	full sun	3a–7b
	Lanceleaf Coreopsis pg. 75	*Coreopsis lanceolata*	full sun	3b–7b
	Little Bluestem pg. 77	*Schizachyrium scoparium*	full sun	3a–7b

ATTRACTS BUTTERFLIES	ATTRACTS BEES	ATTRACTS BIRDS	SOIL PREFERENCE	BLOOM PERIOD	DEER RESISTANCE
yes	no	yes	average–moist	late summer–early fall	yes
yes	yes	yes	average–dry	late spring–early fall	yes
yes	yes	no	moist–wet	spring–midsummer	yes
yes	yes	yes	moist–wet	midsummer–early fall	yes
yes	yes	yes	average–dry	late spring–early summer	yes
yes	yes	yes	average–dry	summer–early fall	yes
yes	yes	yes	average–dry	late spring–midsummer	yes
yes	yes	no	moist–wet	late summer–midfall	yes
yes	yes	no	average–dry	summer–early fall	yes
yes	yes	no	moist	summer	yes
yes	yes	yes	average–moist	midsummer–early fall	yes
yes	yes	yes	average–moist	midsummer–midfall	no
yes	yes	yes	average–dry	midsummer–midfall	no
yes	yes	no	average–moist	late summer–fall	yes
yes	yes	yes	average–moist	midsummer–early fall	yes
yes	no	yes	average	midsummer–early fall	no
yes	yes	yes	average–dry	midsummer–early fall	no
yes	yes	yes	average–dry	midsummer–early fall	yes
yes	yes	yes	average–dry	late spring–midsummer	yes
yes	no	yes	average–dry	late summer–early fall	yes

COMMON NAME	SCIENTIFIC NAME	LIGHT LEVEL	NORTHEAST HARDINESS ZONE
Meadowsweet pg. 79	*Spiraea alba*	full sun	3a–7b
New England Aster pg. 81	*Symphyotrichum novae-angliae*	full sun	3a–7b
Nodding Onion pg. 83	*Allium cernuum*	full sun	3a–7b
Ohio Buckeye pg. 85	*Aesculus glabra*	full sun	3a–7b
Pale Indian Plantain pg. 87	*Arnoglossum atriplicifolium*	full sun	3b–7b
Pickerelweed pg. 89	*Pontederia cordata*	full sun	3a–7b
Purple Coneflower pg. 91	*Echinacea purpurea*	full sun	3a–7b
Queen of the Prairie pg. 93	*Filipendula rubra*	full sun	3a–7b
Roughleaf Dogwood pg. 95	*Cornus drummondii*	full sun	5a–7b
Showy Goldenrod pg. 97	*Solidago speciosa*	full sun	3a–7b
Showy Tick Trefoil pg. 99	*Desmodium canadense*	full sun	3a–7b
Smooth Blue Aster pg. 101	*Symphyotrichum laeve*	full sun	3a–7b
Spotted Joe Pye Weed pg. 103	*Eutrochium maculatum*	full sun	3b–7b
Stiff Goldenrod pg. 105	*Oligoneuron rigidum*	full sun	3a–7b
Swamp Rosemallow pg. 107	*Hibiscus moscheutos*	full sun	5a–7b
Tall Cinquefoil pg. 109	*Drymocallis arguta*	full sun	3a–7b
Trumpet Honeysuckle pg. 111	*Lonicera sempervirens*	full sun	4a–7b
Virginia Mountainmint pg. 113	*Pycnanthemum virginianum*	full sun	3b–7b
Western Pearly Everlasting, pg. 115	*Anaphalis margaritacea*	full sun	3a–7b
Whorled Milkweed pg. 117	*Asclepias verticillata*	full sun	4a–7b
Winged Lythrum pg. 119	*Lythrum alatum*	full sun	3b–7b

ATTRACTS BUTTERFLIES	ATTRACTS BEES	ATTRACTS BIRDS	SOIL PREFERENCE	BLOOM PERIOD	DEER RESISTANCE
yes	yes	yes	moist–wet	midsummer–early fall	yes
yes	yes	yes	average–moist	late summer–midfall	yes
no	yes	no	average	summer	yes
no	yes	yes	moist	spring	yes
no	yes	no	average–dry	midsummer–early fall	yes
yes	yes	hummingbirds	wet	summer–early fall	no
yes	yes	yes	average–dry	summer–early fall	yes
no	yes	no	moist–wet	summer	yes
yes	yes	yes	moist	late spring–early summer	no
yes	yes	yes	average–dry	late summer–fall	yes
yes	yes	no	average–moist	summer–early fall	yes
yes	yes	yes	average–dry	early–late fall	yes
yes	yes	no	moist–wet	midsummer–early fall	yes
yes	yes	no	average	late summer–fall	yes
yes	yes	yes	moist–wet	summer–early fall	no
no	yes	no	average–dry	summer–early fall	moderate
no	no	yes	average–moist	summer–early fall	no
yes	yes	no	average–moist	midsummer–early fall	yes
yes	yes	no	average	summer–fall	yes
yes	yes	no	average–dry	summer–early fall	yes
yes	yes	no	moist–wet	summer–early fall	moderate

FULL SUN TO PARTIAL SHADE

COMMON NAME	SCIENTIFIC NAME	LIGHT LEVEL	NORTHEAST HARDINESS ZONE
Allegheny Serviceberry pg. 123	*Amelanchier laevis*	full sun to partial shade	4a–7b
Alternateleaf Dogwood pg. 125	*Cornus alternifolia*	full sun to partial shade	3a–7b
American Black Elderberry, pg. 127	*Sambucus nigra* ssp. *canadensis*	full sun to partial shade	3a–7b
Black Cherry pg. 129	*Prunus serotina*	full sun to partial shade	3a–7b
Blue Mistflower pg. 131	*Conoclinium coelestinum*	full sun to partial shade	5b–7b
Blue Wild Indigo pg. 133	*Baptisia australis*	full sun to partial shade	3a–7b
Bluebell Bellflower pg. 135	*Campanula rotundifolia*	full sun to partial shade	3a–7b
Brown-Eyed Susan pg. 137	*Rudbeckia triloba*	full sun to partial shade	3b–7b
Burningbush pg. 139	*Euonymus atropurpureus*	full sun to partial shade	3a–7b
Buttonbush pg. 141	*Cephalanthus occidentalis*	full sun to partial shade	4b–7b
Canada Lily pg. 143	*Lilium canadense*	full sun to partial shade	3a–7b
Canada Milkvetch pg. 145	*Astragalus canadensis*	full sun to partial shade	3a–7b
Cardinal Flower pg. 147	*Lobelia cardinalis*	full sun to partial shade	3a–7b
Chokecherry pg. 149	*Prunus virginiana*	full sun to partial shade	2a–7b
Common Boneset pg. 151	*Eupatorium perfoliatum*	full sun to partial shade	3a–7b
Common Evening Primrose, pg. 153	*Oenothera biennis*	full sun to partial shade	4a–7b
Common Hackberry pg. 155	*Celtis occidentalis*	full sun to partial shade	2a–7b
Common Hoptree pg. 157	*Ptelea trifoliata*	full sun to partial shade	3a–7b
Eastern Redbud pg. 159	*Cercis canadensis*	full sun to partial shade	5a–7b
Florida Dogwood pg. 161	*Cornus florida*	full sun to partial shade	5a–7b

ATTRACTS BUTTERFLIES	ATTRACTS BEES	ATTRACTS BIRDS	SOIL PREFERENCE	BLOOM PERIOD	DEER RESISTANCE
yes	yes	yes	moist	midspring	yes
yes	yes	yes	moist	late spring–early summer	moderate
yes	yes	yes	moist	late spring–midsummer	yes
yes	yes	yes	average	spring	no
yes	yes	no	moist	summer–fall	no
yes	yes	yes	dry–moist	late spring–midsummer	yes
yes	yes	no	average–dry	summer	yes
yes	yes	yes	average–moist	midsummer–midfall	yes
no	yes	no	average–moist	late spring–early summer	no
yes	yes	yes	moist–wet	summer	yes
yes	no	yes	moist	late spring–midsummer	no
no	yes	yes	average–moist	summer	no
yes	no	yes	moist	summer–midfall	no
yes	yes	yes	average	spring–early summer	no
yes	yes	no	moist–wet	summer–early fall	yes
moths	yes	yes	average–dry	summer–early fall	moderate
yes	no	yes	moist	spring–early summer	no
yes	yes	yes	average	late spring–early summer	yes
yes	yes	yes	moist	early spring–midspring	yes
yes	yes	yes	average–moist	spring	moderate

29

	COMMON NAME	SCIENTIFIC NAME	LIGHT LEVEL	NORTHEAST HARDINESS ZONE
	Foxglove Beardtongue pg. 163	*Penstemon digitalis*	full sun to partial shade	3a–7b
	Golden Alexanders pg. 165	*Zizia aurea*	full sun to partial shade	3a–7b
	Great Blue Lobelia pg. 167	*Lobelia siphilitica*	full sun to partial shade	4a–7b
	Horseflyweed pg. 169	*Baptisia tinctoria*	full sun to partial shade	3a–7b
	Marsh Marigold pg. 171	*Caltha palustris*	full sun to partial shade	3a–7b
	Maryland Senna pg. 173	*Senna marilandica*	full sun to partial shade	4a–7b
	New Jersey Tea pg. 175	*Ceanothus americanus*	full sun to partial shade	4a–7b
	New York Ironweed pg. 177	*Vernonia noveboracensis*	full sun to partial shade	5a–7b
	Northern Spicebush pg. 179	*Lindera benzoin*	full sun to partial shade	4a–7b
	Obedient Plant pg. 181	*Physostegia virginiana*	full sun to partial shade	3a–7b
	Ohio Spiderwort pg. 183	*Tradescantia ohiensis*	full sun to partial shade	4a–7b
	Partridge Pea pg. 185	*Chamaecrista fasciculata*	full sun to partial shade	3a–7b
	Pawpaw pg. 187	*Asimina triloba*	full sun to partial shade	5a–7b
	Pin Cherry pg. 189	*Prunus pensylvanica*	full sun to partial shade	3a–7b
	Pink Swamp Milkweed pg. 191	*Asclepias incarnata*	full sun to partial shade	3a–7b
	Purplestem Angelica pg. 193	*Angelica atropurpurea*	full sun to partial shade	3b–7b
	Pussy Willow pg. 195	*Salix discolor*	full sun to partial shade	2a–7b
	Red Maple pg. 197	*Acer rubrum*	full sun to partial shade	3a–7b
	Scarlet Beebalm pg. 199	*Monarda didyma*	full sun to partial shade	4a–7b
	Spotted Beebalm pg. 201	*Monarda punctata*	full sun to partial shade	3a–7b
	Spotted Geranium pg. 203	*Geranium maculatum*	full sun to partial shade	3a–7b

ATTRACTS BUTTERFLIES	ATTRACTS BEES	ATTRACTS BIRDS	SOIL PREFERENCE	BLOOM PERIOD	DEER RESISTANCE
yes	yes	yes	average–dry	early–midsummer	yes
yes	yes	no	average–moist	late spring–early summer	yes
yes	yes	yes	moist–wet	summer–fall	no
yes	yes	no	average–dry	late spring–early summer	yes
no	yes	yes	moist–wet	midspring–early summer	yes
yes	yes	yes	average–moist	summer–early fall	yes
yes	yes	yes	average–dry	spring	no
yes	yes	yes	moist	late summer–early fall	yes
yes	yes	yes	moist	early spring	no
yes	yes	yes	average–moist	midsummer–early fall	yes
no	yes	no	dry–moist	spring–summer	no
yes	yes	yes	average–dry	summer–early fall	no
yes	no	no	moist	spring	yes
yes	yes	yes	average–moist	late spring–early summer	yes
yes	yes	yes	moist	summer–early fall	yes
yes	yes	no	moist–wet	spring–summer	yes
yes	yes	yes	moist–wet	spring	yes
moths	yes	yes	moist	early spring	no
yes	yes	yes	average–moist	midsummer–early fall	yes
yes	yes	yes	dry	midsummer–early fall	yes
yes	yes	yes	moist	spring–early summer	yes

	COMMON NAME	SCIENTIFIC NAME	LIGHT LEVEL	NORTHEAST HARDINESS ZONE
	Swamp Rose pg. 205	*Rosa palustris*	full sun to partial shade	4a–7b
	Turk's-Cap Lily pg. 207	*Lilium superbum*	full sun to partial shade	5a–7b
	White Turtlehead pg. 209	*Chelone glabra*	full sun to partial shade	3a–7b
	Wild Bergamot pg. 211	*Monarda fistulosa*	full sun to partial shade	3a–7b
	Wild Lupine pg. 213	*Lupinus perennis*	full sun to partial shade	3a–7b
	Wild Sweetwilliam pg. 215	*Phlox maculata*	full sun to partial shade	3a–7b

PARTIAL SHADE TO FULL SHADE

	COMMON NAME	SCIENTIFIC NAME	LIGHT LEVEL	NORTHEAST HARDINESS ZONE
	Bigleaf Aster pg. 219	*Eurybia macrophylla*	partial shade to full shade	3a–7b
	Black Baneberry pg. 221	*Actaea racemosa*	partial shade to full shade	3a–7b
	Canada Anemone pg. 223	*Anemone canadensis* (also *A. virginiana*)	partial shade to full shade	2a–7b
	Common Blue Violet pg. 225	*Viola sororia*	partial shade to full shade	3a–7b
	Common Pricklyash pg. 227	*Zanthoxylum americanum*	partial shade to full shade	3a–7b
	Cutleaf Coneflower pg. 229	*Rudbeckia laciniata*	partial shade to full shade	3a–7b
	Eastern Waterleaf pg. 231	*Hydrophyllum virginianum*	partial shade to full shade	4a–7b
	Feathery False Lily of the Valley, pg. 233	*Maianthemum racemosum*	partial shade to full shade	3a–7b
	Hairy Pagoda-Plant pg. 235	*Blephilia hirsuta*	partial shade to full shade	4a–7b
	Jewelweed pg. 237	*Impatiens capensis*	partial shade to full shade	2a–7b
	Purple Milkweed pg. 239	*Asclepias purpurascens*	partial shade to full shade	4a–7b
	Red Columbine pg. 241	*Aquilegia canadensis*	partial shade to full shade	3a–7b
	Smallspike False Nettle pg. 243	*Boehmeria cylindrica*	partial shade to full shade	3b–7b
	Smooth Solomon's Seal pg. 245	*Polygonatum biflorum*	partial shade to full shade	3b–7b

ATTRACTS BUTTERFLIES	ATTRACTS BEES	ATTRACTS BIRDS	SOIL PREFERENCE	BLOOM PERIOD	DEER RESISTANCE
yes	yes	yes	moist–wet	summer	no
yes	no	yes	moist	early summer–midsummer	no
yes	yes	yes	moist–wet	summer–early fall	yes
yes	yes	yes	dry–moist	summer–early fall	yes
yes	yes	yes	average–dry	late spring–early summer	no
yes	no	yes	average–moist	summer–early fall	yes
yes	yes	yes	average–moist	late summer–fall	no
yes	yes	yes	moist	early summer–midsummer	yes
no	yes	no	moist	late spring–early summer	yes
yes	yes	no	moist	spring	yes
yes	yes	yes	average–moist	spring	yes
yes	yes	yes	moist	midsummer–early fall	yes
no	yes	no	average–moist	late spring–early summer	no
no	yes	yes	average–moist	late spring–early summer	moderate
yes	yes	no	moist	summer	yes
yes	yes	yes	moist–wet	summer–fall	moderate
yes	yes	yes	average–moist	summer	yes
yes	yes	yes	average–moist	spring–early summer	yes
yes	no	no	average–moist	summer	no
no	yes	yes	average–wet	late spring–early summer	yes

Northeast Plants at a Glance (continued)

	COMMON NAME	SCIENTIFIC NAME	LIGHT LEVEL	NORTHEAST HARDINESS ZONE
	Sweetscented Joe Pye Weed, pg. 247	*Eutrochium purpureum*	partial shade to full shade	4a–7b
	Virginia Bluebells pg. 249	*Mertensia virginica*	partial shade to full shade	3a–7b
	Virginia Snakeroot pg. 251	*Aristolochia serpentaria*	partial shade to full shade	5a–7b
	White Snakeroot pg. 253	*Ageratina altissima*	partial shade to full shade	3a–7b
	Wild Blue Phlox pg. 255	*Phlox divaricata*	partial shade to full shade	3a–7b
	Woodland Sunflower pg. 257	*Helianthus divaricatus*	partial shade to full shade	3a–7b
	Zigzag Goldenrod pg. 259	*Solidago flexicaulis*	partial shade to full shade	3a–7b

Scarlet Beebalm

ATTRACTS BUTTERFLIES	ATTRACTS BEES	ATTRACTS BIRDS	SOIL PREFERENCE	BLOOM PERIOD	DEER RESISTANCE
yes	yes	no	moist	midsummer–early fall	yes
yes	yes	yes	moist	spring	yes
yes	no	no	moist	late spring–early summer	yes
yes	yes	no	moist	late summer–fall	yes
yes	yes	yes	moist	spring	yes
yes	yes	yes	average–dry	midsummer–early fall	no
yes	yes	yes	average–moist	late summer–fall	yes

Common Milkweed

Common Ninebark

Full Sun

Culver's Root

Lanceleaf Coreopsis

Pickerelweed

Garden Phlox

Butterflyweed

Black-Eyed Susan

From New England Aster (page 81) to Showy Goldenrod (page 97), some of the plants we associate most with pollinators and hummingbirds thrive in full sun. These plants require at least 6 hours of direct sunlight, but that's the minimum. In many cases, they produce larger and more copious blooms if they have more than 8 hours of sunlight—especially during the afternoon hours, when the sun is at its strongest.

Purple Coneflower

Hoary Vervain

Big Bluestem

Scientific Name *Andropogon gerardii*

Family Poaceae

Plant Characteristics Upright, clump-forming perennial grass up to 7 feet tall; long, narrow, bluish-green to green leaves; terminal, 3-branched, reddish-purple, tassel-like flowers.

USDA Hardiness Zones 4a–7b

Bloom Period Late summer–early fall

Growing Conditions Performs best in full sun and organically rich, average to moist, well-drained soils.

Aptly named, Big Bluestem is a tall, clump-forming native grass of meadows and open woods. . Impressive in stature, mature plants typically dwarf those of many other native grasses, adding both height and soft texture to the landscape. Plants spread by underground rhizomes and can quickly form larger colonies. It's well suited for naturalizing in wildflower meadows or clustered together with flowering perennials as a prominent accent or backdrop. Highly adaptable to most soil conditions, it is easy to grow, requires limited maintenance, and is quite drought tolerant once established. In late summer, the tops of the plants are adorned with distinctive, three-branched flower heads that are said to resemble the shape of a wild turkey's foot. The foliage takes on a coppery-red color as autumn progresses, with the rich tones lingering through the winter months. In more ornamental spaces, gardeners may wish to cut the old growth back to the ground in spring to provide a neater appearance and help new foliage to emerge.

Attracts butterflies; serves as a larval host for the Arogos Skipper (Atrytone arogos), *Cobweb Skipper* (Hesperia metea), *Common Wood Nymph* (Cercyonis pegala), *Delaware Skipper* (Anatrytone logan), *and Dusted Skipper* (Atrytonopsis hianna); *provides cover for birds and small mammals.*

Black-Eyed Susan

Scientific Name *Rudbeckia hirta*

Family Asteraceae

Plant Characteristics Upright biennial or short-lived perennial (lasting a few years) 1–3 feet tall; leaves are coarse and green; daisylike flowers are yellow, with dark-brown to black centers atop stiff, slender stems.

USDA Hardiness Zones 3a–7b

Bloom Period Late spring–early fall

Growing Conditions Performs best in full sun and average to dry, well-drained soils. It is highly adaptable to a wide range of soil types and conditions.

This cheerful and somewhat old-fashioned wildflower is a favorite of many gardeners. A fast-growing and tough-as-nails native, it can tolerate drought, heat, and poor soils. Fertile conditions and regular moisture will enhance growth and performance. Black-Eyed Susan is equally easy to propagate by seed and readily blooms in the first year. Ideal for perennial borders, cottage gardens (small, informal, densely packed gardens), or naturalizing, it produces a prolonged floral display and is a terrific pollinator attractor, drawing in a wide array of different insects. It also makes a great cut flower. Deadheading spent flowers will encourage reblooming. While generally short-lived and often grown like an annual, the plants readily reseed and tend to pop up again year after year. Several commercial cultivars are also available.

Attracts butterflies, bees, wasps, and many other insect pollinators; serves as larval host for the Silvery Checkerspot Butterfly (Chlosyne nycteis) and Wavy-Lined Emerald Moth (Synchlora aerata); songbirds feed on the seeds.

Blue Flag Iris

Scientific Name *Iris virginica*

Family Iridaceae

Plant Characteristics Upright, herbaceous perennial up to 3 feet tall; long, straplike, green leaves overlap at the base; broad, spreading, violet-blue flowers have large, downward-curving sepals with prominent yellow patches and noticeable dark veining.

USDA Hardiness Zones 4a–7b

Bloom Period Spring–midsummer

Growing Conditions Performs best in full sun and organically rich, moist to wet soils.

Also called Virginia Iris, this distinctive wildflower is a true wetland species. It is often encountered in marshes, damp woodlands, and along pond or stream margins. The shallow-rooted, leafy plants thrive in rich organic soil and can tolerate shallow standing water. While an obvious choice for rain and water gardens, Blue Flag Iris will perform well in more-traditional perennial beds if the soil is kept consistently moist and is never allowed to fully dry out. Individual plants expand into larger clumps over time and can spread by rhizomes to form colonies. The long, swordlike leaves orient upwards from the base, creating an attractive display that adds both texture and interest. Early-season bloomers, the broad, arching flowers each regularly measure more than 3 inches across.

Attracts butterflies and larger bees.

Blue Vervain

Scientific Name *Verbena hastata*

Family Verbenaceae

Plant Characteristics Slender, upright, herbaceous perennial up to 5 feet tall; long, lance-shaped, green leaves have serrated margins; terminal, branched, narrow, spikelike clusters of tubular, lobed, violet-blue flowers sit atop stiff, square, somewhat reddish stems.

USDA Hardiness Zones 3a–7b

Bloom Period Midsummer–early fall

Growing Conditions Full sun and moist to wet, organically rich, well-drained soils.

Blue Vervain is a common wetland wildflower that thrives in moist, soggy conditions. It is an excellent addition to wet meadows; pond or stream margins; rain gardens; and other damp, habitually sunny locations. The plant spreads readily by underground rhizomes and self-seeding, leading to the rapid formation of larger colonies; as a result, it can be a bit aggressive for smaller garden sites but is ideal for naturalizing. Plants produce terminal, branched arrangements of long spikes, reminiscent of a small candelabra, that bloom from the bottom up. The individual tubular flowers, while small, are densely packed and open progressively up the narrow spike, only a few at a time. The resulting display is quite visually attractive, especially when planted in larger groupings or in combination with other moisture-loving perennials such as Sweetscented Joe Pye Weed (page 247), Common Boneset (page 151), and Pink Swamp Milkweed (page 191).

Attracts butterflies, bees, wasps, and many other insect pollinators; songbirds eat the seeds.

Butterflyweed

Scientific Name *Asclepias tuberosa*

Family Apocynaceae

Plant Characteristics Upright, herbaceous perennial up to 2 feet tall; green leaves are narrow and oblong; flat, terminal clusters of light-orange to deep-reddish-orange flowers grow on terminally branched, hairy stems. The plant forms compact, multistemmed, and somewhat arching clumps over time. Plants have deep taproots and cannot easily be transplanted.

USDA Hardiness Zones 3a–7b

Bloom Period Late spring–early summer

Growing Conditions Perfroms best in full sun and average to dry, well-drained soils. Drought and heat tolerant once established, it does well in poor soils. Often best cultivated from seed.

Aptly named, this stunning native perennial is an absolute butterfly favorite. Its showy clusters of vivid orange flowers demand attention in any landscape and are highly enticing to a broad range of insect pollinators. Perfect in sunny, dry locations, Butterflyweed is a welcome addition to gardens of all sizes and styles, from smaller, more-formal perennial borders to expansive, naturalized meadows and open woodlands. It is relatively easy to grow but requires well-drained soils. Over time, plants form compact, multistemmed, and somewhat arching clumps, as well as deep taproots that make them quite tolerant of drought but almost impossible to transplant easily. Elongated, spindle-shaped seedpods form after flowering; when mature, they split open to release numerous silky, tufted seeds that readily disperse by wind.

Attracts butterflies, bees, and other insect pollinators, as well as hummingbirds; serves as a larval host for the Monarch Butterfly (Danaus plexippus).

Common Milkweed

Scientific Name *Asclepias syriaca*

Family Apocynaceae

Plant Characteristics Upright, herbaceous perennial up to 5 feet tall (or taller); large, oblong, green leaves bear rounded clusters of pale-pink to lavender flowers.

USDA Hardiness Zones 3a–7b

Bloom Period Summer–early fall

Growing Conditions Prefers full sun and average to dry, well-drained soils. Tolerant of poor soils and drought.

This native perennial is one of the most widespread and common milkweeds in the Northeast. A key larval host for the Monarch Butterfly, Common Milkweed is a plant of open areas such as roadsides, fencerows, woodland borders, and old fields. An aggressive colonizer of disturbed sites, it spreads by both underground rhizomes and airborne seeds, forming extensive colonies. As a result, it has a tendency to get weedy and overtake smaller garden areas. Easy to grow and fast to establish, plants are tolerant of poor soil, drought, and neglect. Despite its weedy habit, it is a worthy addition to gardens and larger naturalized plantings. A profuse bloomer, the large, rounded flower clusters perfume the air with a delightful fragrance and are exceptionally attractive to butterflies, sphinx moths, beetles, bees, and many other insect pollinators. Later in the season, the flowers give rise to large, elongated, somewhat spiny seedpods that split open at maturity to release copious amounts of silky, tufted seeds that spread via the wind. The old seedpods remain well into winter.

Very attractive to butterflies, bees, and other insect pollinators, as well as hummingbirds; serves as an important larval host plant for the Monarch Butterfly (Danaus plexippus).

Common Ninebark

Scientific Name *Physocarpus opulifolius*

Family Rosaceae

Plant Characteristics Deciduous shrub up to 10 feet tall; lobed, oval to lance-shaped, dark-green leaves grow on woody branches with exfoliating brown bark; 5-petaled white flowers grow in rounded, terminal clusters.

USDA Hardiness Zones 2a–7b

Bloom Period Late spring–midsummer

Growing Conditions Full sun and average to dry, well-drained soils.

A fast-growing and exceptionally hardy native shrub, Common Ninebark provides year-round beauty and high wildlife value. Plants are quite adaptable to a range of soil conditions and tolerant of drought once established. They have an attractive, mounding growth habit, with spreading branches and distinctive exfoliating bark that offer much winter interest. In early summer, plants produce dense, rounded clusters of showy white flowers, which provide abundant pollen and nectar resources for a broad range of insect pollinators. Nevertheless, Common Ninebark remains underappreciated for its pollinator attraction. The blooms are followed by conspicuous, pinkish-brown seed capsules, which are eaten by some songbirds, and leaves that take on showy fall colors. This plant is a wonderful addition to any garden, whether as a hedge, an individual specimen, or clustered together for a more naturalistic effect. Numerous cultivars are available that vary in both form and leaf color, offering additional ornamental options.

Attracts butterflies, bees, flies, and other pollinators; seeds provide food for some songbirds; the dense plants offer cover and nesting sites for songbirds.

Common Sneezeweed

Scientific Name *Helenium autumnale*

Family Asteraceae

Plant Characteristics Upright, clump-forming, herbaceous perennial up to 5 feet tall; long, lance-shaped to elliptical, dark-green leaves have serrated margins on stout, branching distinctively winged stems; terminal clusters of golden-yellow, daisylike flowers each have 3 bright-yellow, lobed rays surrounding a prominently domed, darker golden center.

USDA Hardiness Zones 3a–7b

Bloom Period Late summer–midfall

Growing Conditions Full sun and moist to wet, organically rich soils.

Widespread across the United States from Massachusetts to California and south to Florida, this plant gets its common name from a Menominee Indian practice of crushing dried leaves to produce sneezing, which they believed to be conducive to health. But in a garden setting, this flower is a delightful wetland perennial, and it won't provoke a trip to the pharmacy for allergy medication. A late-season bloomer, the plant has bright-yellow, toothed, wedge-shaped petals surrounding a central domed, golden-bronze cone, adding a profusion of autumnal color to the landscape. Common Sneezeweed is a plant of open wetlands, pond and stream margins, wet ditches, and other soggy sites, and is thus intolerant of prolonged drought. Plants are easy to grow and adaptable to sunny garden settings, thriving with regular moisture and fertile soils. Attractive individually or en masse, it is a welcome addition to a rain garden or well-irrigated perennial border; it's also good for naturalizing in larger wet meadows or perpetually moist areas. Numerous highly attractive ornamental cultivars are available.

Attracts butterflies, bees, and many other insect pollinators.

Common Yarrow

Scientific Name *Achillea millefolium*

Family Asteraceae

Plant Characteristics Upright to somewhat mat-forming perennial up to 3 feet tall; highly dissected, ferny, bright-green leaves; dense, flat-topped clusters of small, white flowers (may vary to slightly pink in color) with creamy or pale-yellow centers sit atop upright, terminally branched, leafy stems.

Hardiness Zone 3a–7b

Bloom Period Summer–early fall

Growing Conditions Performs best in full sun and average to dry, well-drained soils.

In spite of its delicate appearance, Common Yarrow is a tough, low-maintenance perennial. It is easy to cultivate and highly adaptable to a variety of garden soils with good drainage; it's also tolerant of both heat and drought. Highly attractive in either natural and formal landscapes, it makes an excellent addition to rock gardens, perennial borders, and larger open meadows, or even planted as a flowering ground cover. It works well alongside other sun-loving perennials such as Black-Eyed Susan (page 41), Purple Coneflower (page 91), Wild Bergamot (page 211), and Butterflyweed (page 47). Common Yarrow spreads by underground rhizomes and can be quite aggressive, forming large, matlike colonies over time. Plants can be divided regularly to help curb growth. The long-lasting blooms attract a wide range of pollinating insects and also make great cut flowers. The species' presence in North America represents a complex of both native and introduced stock from Europe and Asia. A number of different cultivars are commercially available, including several varieties in different colors.

Highly attractive to butterflies, bees, wasps, and many other insect pollinators.

Culver's Root

Scientific Name *Veronicastrum virginicum*

Family Scrophulariaceae

Plant Characteristics Upright, herbaceous perennial up to 6 feet tall; oval green leaves with serrated margins are whorled and scattered along sturdy green stems, with elongated, dense, terminal to axillary spikes of small, white, tubular flowers.

USDA Hardiness Zones 3a–7b

Bloom Period Summer

Growing Conditions Full sun and moist, organically rich, well-drained soils.

This striking native adds elements of elegance and verticality to the landscape. Each sturdy stem bears widely spaced, whorled leaves that give the plant an airy appearance overall. Slender spikes of small, tubular flowers, many reaching 6 inches or more in length, begin to appear in early- to midsummer. Additional smaller, branched, lateral spikes result in a broad, eye-catching terminal arrangement that somewhat resembles a candelabra. The showy blooms draw in a wide range of flower-visiting insects. Culver's Root is a distinctive addition to sunny wetland edges, moist meadows, rain gardens, or the back of perennial borders. The plant is long-lasting under ideal conditions but is intolerant of prolonged drought. It is particularly attractive if planted alongside other colorful, moisture-loving perennials such as Blue Vervain (page 45), Pink Swamp Milkweed (page 191), and Spotted Joe Pye Weed (page 103). Several cultivars are commercially available.

Attracts butterflies, bees, and many other insect pollinators.

Cup Plant

Scientific Name *Silphium perfoliatum*

Family Asteraceae

Plant Characteristics Stout, upright, herbaceous perennial up to 9 feet tall; large, somewhat triangular, clasping green leaves have toothed margins; smooth, sturdy, somewhat squarish stems bear loose, branched, terminal clusters of large, bright-yellow, sunflower-like flowers.

Hardiness Zone 3a–7b

Bloom Period Midsummer–early fall

Growing Conditions Full sun and average to moist, organically rich, well-drained soils.

This durable native is yet another truly unique and impressively stately plant found sporadically throughout the Northeast. Cup Plant is named its large, clasping eaves, which are fused to each other at the base around the central stem to form a basin that can actually hold rainwater. Plants expand into imposing, multistemmed clumps that produce expansive terminal arrays of golden blooms later in the season. The striking plants add texture and height to the landscape, soaring well over human height. The large, copious blooms are readily visited by butterflies, bees, and other flower-loving insects. Plants spread vigorously by underground rhizomes and can rapidly expand into larger colonies. Like other members of the genus *Silphium*, this native is easy to cultivate, long-lived, and quite durable once established.

Attracts butterflies, bees, and other insect pollinators; songbirds feed on the seeds and may occasionally sip water from the plant's natural "cups."

Dense Blazing Star

Scientific Name *Liatris spicata*

Family Asteraceae

Plant Characteristics Upright, clump-forming, herbaceous perennial up to 5 feet tall, with long, dense, grasslike, green basal leaves and dense, elongated, spikelike clusters of small, tubular pink flowers.

USDA Hardiness Zones 3a–7b

Bloom Period Midsummer–midfall

Growing Conditions Full sun and organically rich, average to moist, well-drained soils.

Arguably the most commercially available type of blazing star, this clump-forming perennial is a common addition to perennial borders, cottage gardens, rain gardens, or pollinator gardens. Also called Marsh Blazing Star, it thrives in sunny, moist sites and wetland margins but can be easily grown in rich garden soil if regular moisture is provided. It is also a superb species for naturalizing and looks particularly spectacular when planted en masse. Dense Blazing Star boasts attractive, mounding, grasslike foliage that is perfect for creating soft texture in the landscape. Later in the summer, plants produce stout stems that terminate in elongated, wandlike spikes, some approaching 2 feet in length. These spikes bloom from the top down, yielding an explosion of pink flowers that are favorites of butterflies, bees, and hummingbirds. Numerous commercial cultivars are readily available that vary in color and form. Several other native blazing star species occur throughout the region, including Devil's Bite (page 63). These differ somewhat in their habitat preferences and general overall appearance, but all are pollinator magnets and worthy of attention.

Attracts hummingbirds, butterflies, bees, and other insect pollinators; songbirds feed on the seeds.

Devil's Bite

Scientific Name *Liatris scariosa*

Family Asteraceae

Plant Characteristics Upright, clump-forming, unbranched herbaceous perennial up to 4 feet tall (or slightly taller); dense, long, lance-shaped to elliptical, green basal leaves become smaller and more linear up the stem; terminal, elongated, spikelike clusters of dense, fuzzy flower heads on short stalks up the stem, with each cluster composed of many small, tubular, pink flowers.

Hardiness Zone 3a–7b

Bloom Period Midsummer–midfall

Growing Conditions Full sun and average to dry, well-drained soil.

Despite its diabolical name, Devil's Bite is an extremely handsome and garden-worthy blazing star. It is typically found in savannas and dry, open woodlands with somewhat sandy to rocky soils. Plants are nonetheless quite adaptable to more organically rich conditions with extra moisture; they can even tolerate light shade. Devil's Bite makes a wonderful addition to perennial bogs, butterfly gardens, or larger meadows or naturalized areas. Like other blazing stars, it has dense, narrow leaves that add a softer texture to the landscape. Over time, plants expand into sizable clumps. Starting in mid to late summer, Devil's Bite sends up tall, nearly 2-foot-long inflorescences that show-case dozens of individually stalked, buttonlike pink flowerheads scattered along the stem. The resulting display is quite striking and a huge draw for foraging insects. It is particularly attractive to Monarch Butterflies, which seek nectar-rich blooms to help fuel their south-ward fall migration. The plants are easily grown and require little maintenance outside of occasional staking to help keep the flowering stalks from falling over.

Attracts hummingbirds, butterflies, bees, and other insect pollinators; songbirds feed on the seeds.

False Aster

Scientific Name *Boltonia asteroides*

Family Asteraceae

Plant Characteristics Upright, herbaceous perennial up to 5 feet tall; narrow, lance-shaped green leaves become shorter up the plant; terminal, branched clusters of small, bright, white, daisylike flowers have yellow centers.

Hardiness Zone 3a–7b

Bloom Period Late summer–fall

Growing Conditions Full sun and average to moist, well-drained soils.

This handsome and underutilized perennial develops into sizable multistemmed clumps over time, but it is not aggressive in garden situations. While it thrives in organically rich, moist soils, False Aster is highly adaptable to a variety of conditions, enduring both periodic drought and standing water. In late summer, the plants begin to burst forth with a profuse array of small, brilliant white flowers. The resulting snowdrift-like effect is impressive, often earning this native the nickname of "thousand-flowered aster." A wide variety of pollinators, from butterflies and bees to wasps and beetles, takes advantage of the abundant floral resources. Plants provide a showy pop of white to a late-season landscape traditionally dominated by yellows and purples. A sound choice for the perennial border, cottage garden, or pollinator garden, either individually or in larger drifts, False Aster is equally useful for naturalizing in meadows or in larger open spaces.

Attracts butterflies, bees, and other insect pollinators.

Field Thistle

Scientific Name *Cirsium discolor*

Family Asteraceae

Plant Characteristics Upright biennial or short-lived perennial to 7 feet in height or slightly more; long, sharply lobed and spiny green leaves on stout, hairy but not spiny stems; large dome-like light-pink flower heads subtended by scaly green bracts.

Hardiness Zone 3a–7b

Bloom Period Midsummer–early fall

Growing Conditions Full sun and average to moist soils.

Despite often being misconstrued as an undesirable weed, our native Field Thistle is in fact an outstanding wildlife-attracting and supporting wildflower. It, unlike various non-native thistles, is not invasive and will not displace native vegetation or readily overrun landscapes. Instead, the stately plants offer much interest and attention. The spiny leaves are green above but a light powdery grayish below and certainly demand caution (and sturdy gloves) when handling or working nearby. Starting in midsummer, the plants produce large fuzzy flower heads that are exceptionally attractive to pollinators, large and small. Butterflies and bees in particular are frequent visitors. When finished blooming, the heads explode, releasing the fluffy, silk-laden seed to be readily dispersed by the wind. Also called Pasture Thistle, it is easily grown and quite accommodating of various soils. Thriving in full sun, the plants are perfect for more-wild, native landscapes or a unique addition to a butterfly garden.

Attracts butterflies, bees, beetles, flies, sphinx moths and hummingbirds; serves as a larval host for the Painted Lady Butterfly (Vanessa cardui); various songbirds consume the seeds.

Garden Phlox

Scientific Name *Phlox paniculata*

Family Polemoniaceae

Plant Characteristics Upright, clump-forming, herbaceous perennial up to 4 feet tall (or slightly taller); narrow, elliptical, dark-green leaves have pointed tips oppositely arranged on sturdy, smooth, unbranched stems; large, dense, and somewhat rounded or domed terminal clusters of trumpet-shaped, tubular flowers are various colors including pink, magenta, lavender, or white.

Hardiness Zone 4a–7b

Bloom Period Midsummer–early fall

Growing Conditions Performs best in full sun and average-moisture, organically rich, well-drained soils.

Also called Summer Phlox, this showy native perennial is a popular staple of many perennial and cottage gardens. This sun-loving species thrives in fertile soils with regular moisture and is intolerant of prolonged drought. Too much moisture and poor air circulation can lead to problems, including powdery mildew. Given the right conditions, though, plants quickly expand to sizable, multistemmed clumps. Beginning in midsummer, Garden Phlox bursts forth with impressive clusters of fragrant, five-lobed flowers that vary considerably in color. Many additional color cultivars are available, as well as several that are mildew resistant. Garden Phlox makes an excellent cut flower, has a long bloom period, and quickly draws in hummingbirds and butterflies. Beyond traditional flower bed use, it helps brighten up woodland edges. Deadheading spent flower heads will promote reblooming.

Attracts butterflies, sphinx moths, and hummingbirds.

Hairy Lespedeza

Scientific Name *Lespedeza hirta*

Family Fabaceae

Plant Characteristics Herbaceous perennial up to 3 feet tall; compound, cloverlike, hairy, green leaves have 3 oval leaflets; compact, spikelike clusters of small, pealike, cream-colored flowers are marked with purple.

Hardiness Zone 4b–7b

Bloom Period Midsummer–early fall

Growing Conditions Full sun and average to dry, well-drained soils.

A widespread wildflower of dry woodlands, savannas, and adjacent semiopen habitats, Hairy Lespedeza won't win over many gardeners with its overall attractiveness. Nonetheless, it provides many wildlife benefits in the form of floral resources and larval food. The wiry plants are sparingly branched and display namesake hairy stems and leaves. Numerous short inflorescences showcase small, pealike, purple-accented blooms that are regularly visited by native bees. Like other legumes, these plants fix atmospheric nitrogen into the soil. Also called Hairy Bush Clover, this species is tough and adaptable, but it's probably best used in informal, naturalistic landscapes.

Attracts butterflies and bees; serves as a larval host for Silver-Spotted Skipper (Epargyreus clarus)*, Northern Cloudywing* (Thorybes pylades)*, and Southern Cloudywing* (Thorybes bathyllus) *Butterflies; songbirds consume the seeds.*

Hoary Vervain

Scientific Name *Verbena stricta*

Family Verbenaceae

Plant Characteristics Upright, clump-forming, herbaceous perennial up to 4 feet tall; oval, hairy, gray-green leaves have serrated margins on hairy, square, green to reddish-green stems; dense, slender, terminal spikes have 5-lobed, tubular, purple-blue flowers.

Hardiness Zone 3a–7b

Bloom Period Midsummer–early fall

Growing Conditions Full sun and average to dry, well-drained soils.

This unique wildflower is considerably underutilized in most landscapes. A short-lived perennial, it is easy to grow and thrives in dry sites with poor soils. While plants readily reseed, they do not become weedy or aggressive in the landscape. As a result, Hoary Vervain can be a sound choice for naturalizing; however, it is equally useful for incorporation into a perennial border or smaller flower bed. The leaves and stems are noticeably covered with fine hairs that give the plant an overall soft, grayish-green, hoary appearance. Its elongated flower spikes bloom from the bottom up, with the resulting ½-inch-wide flowers producing a showy and relatively long-lasting display during the latter half of summer and into early fall. Like the similar-looking Blue Vervain, Hoary Vervain attracts a wide range of insects, including many native bees and butterflies.

Attracts butterflies, bees, and many other insect pollinators, as well as hummingbirds; many songbirds and small mammals feed on the seeds.

Lanceleaf Coreopsis

Scientific Name *Coreopsis lanceolata*

Family Asteraceae

Plant Characteristics Compact, clump-forming, herbaceous perennial to 2 feet in height; elongated, lance-shaped, green basal leaves become smaller and deeply lobed up the stems; bright golden-yellow, daisylike flower heads each have lobed yellow rays surrounding a golden center, atop erect, slender, green stems.

USDA Hardiness Zones 3b–7b

Bloom Period Late spring–midsummer

Growing Conditions Performs best in full sun and average to dry, well-drained soils.

This delightfully cheery perennial is a favorite of many gardeners. A common addition to wildflower seed mixes, Lanceleaf Coreopsis is an excellent choice for naturalizing in meadows, along roadsides or utility easements, or in other open landscapes. Plants freely self-seed and can quickly spread to form extensive colonies. Plants have a compact growth habit that is ideal for smaller gardens, perennial borders, and container plantings. Exceptionally durable, adaptable, and easy to grow, Lanceleaf Coreopsis thrives in sunny, well-drained sites and is quite tolerant of heat, drought, humidity, and neglect once established. Naturalized plantings can even tolerate periodic mowing. Plants produce profusions of showy yellow flowers that are beloved by a wide variety of insect pollinators. Numerous ornamental cultivars are available commercially.

Attracts butterflies, bees, and other insect pollinators; serves as a larval host for the Wavy-Lined Emerald Moth (Synchlora aerata); songbirds and small mammals eat the seeds.

Little Bluestem

Scientific Name *Schizachyrium scoparium*

Family Poaceae

Plant Characteristics Upright, perennial grass up to 4 feet tall; leaves are dense, narrow, bluish-green, spiky, linear; flowers (spikelets) are elongated, erect, purplish.

USDA Hardiness Zones 3a–7b

Bloom Period Late summer–early fall

Growing Conditions Full sun and average to dry, well-drained soils.

This upright, clump-forming grass occurs in many open to semi-open habitats. For landscape use, it offers outstanding ornamental and wildlife value year-round. As its name suggests, Little Bluestem has showy, fine-textured, bluish-green foliage and a dense, mounding growth habit. It is ideal for naturalizing, for grouping together en masse, or as an accent with flowering perennials. Later in summer, plants produce attractive but somewhat inconspicuous purplish flowers that are soon followed by fuzzy, silvery seed heads that persist into early winter. The real show, however, starts in fall, when the foliage transitions to a rich copper-burgundy color, providing wonderful dormant-season interest. Easily grown and quite hardy, Little Bluestem accommodates a range of soil conditions but is intolerant of excessive moisture.

Attracts butterflies; serves as a larval host for several butterflies, including the Cobweb Skipper (Hesperia metea), Common Wood Nymph (Cercyonis pegala), Crossline Skipper (Polites origenes), Dusted Skipper (Atrytonopsis hianna), Indian Skipper (Hesperia sassacus), Leonard's Skipper (Hesperia leonardus), and Swarthy Skipper (Nastra lherminier); songbirds feed on the seeds; provides cover for birds and other wildlife.

Meadowsweet

Scientific Name *Spiraea alba*

Family Rosaceae

Plant Characteristics Upright deciduous shrub up to 5 feet tall (or slightly taller); narrow, dark, oblong to lance-shaped green leaves have sharply toothed margins on upright, unbranched stems; 5-petaled, fuzzy white flowers grow in dense, terminal, wand-shaped clusters.

USDA Hardiness Zones 3a–7b

Bloom Period Midsummer–early fall

Growing Conditions Full sun and moist to wet, organically rich, well-drained soils.

This multistemmed shrub thrives in sunny, wet sites and is at home in swamps, damp meadows, or along streams or other wetland margins. While often best used in these native or wildlife landscapes, it can be grown in organically rich garden soils with regular irrigation. At first glance, the numerous slender green branches often resemble those of a perennial but become brown and woody with age. Meadowsweet spreads by suckering and can form small thickets over time. For smaller spaces, trim suckers regularly to constrain expansion. Later in summer, the plant produces dense, elongated terminal clusters of white flowers that have long stamens and give the entire inflorescence a noticeably fuzzy appearance. The copious blooms are frequently visited by butterflies, bees, and a wide range of other insect pollinators.

Attracts butterflies, bees, and other insect pollinators; serves as a larval host for Northern Azure (Celastrina lucia) *and Spring Azure* (Celastrina ladon) *Butterflies; songbirds often consume the seeds; provides cover and nesting sites for various songbirds and game birds.*

New England Aster

Scientific Name *Symphyotrichum novae-angliae*

Family Asteraceae

Plant Characteristics Upright, clump-forming, herbaceous perennial to 5 feet tall (or slightly taller); narrow, hairy, clasping, lance-shaped to oblong, green to gray-green leaves grow on hairy, reddish-brown stems; extensive terminal clusters of daisylike flowers are purple with yellow centers.

USDA Hardiness Zones 3a–7b

Bloom Period Late summer–midfall

Growing Conditions Full sun and average to moist, organically rich, well-drained soils.

A true harbinger of autumn, this stunning perennial is a must-have for any northern garden. It's easy to cultivate in sunny garden sites with regular moisture and good air circulation, but it's not overly tolerant of heat or drought. The robust clumps produce several sturdy, erect stems that are encircled by hairy, distinctively clasping leaves. As fall approaches, New England Aster produces a profusion of magnificent blooms that range in color from deep purple to pink, highlighted by golden-yellow centers. While particularly showy en masse in meadow landscapes, individual plants or groupings add verticality and bright, rich hues to any cottage garden or perennial bed. For a particularly majestic effect, combine with goldenrods (*Solidago* spp.), rudbeckias (*Rudbeckia* spp.), sunflowers (*Helianthus* spp.), or other yellow-flowered perennials. Beloved by pollinators, the plentiful blooms represent a critical late-season resource for migrating Monarch Butterflies and many other flower-visiting insects.

Attracts butterflies, bees, and other pollinators; songbirds feed on the seeds.

Nodding Onion

Scientific Name *Allium cernuum*

Family Amaryllidaceae

Plant Characteristics Small, perennial bulb up to 1½ feet tall; green leaves are long, narrow, grasslike; star-shaped, whitish or light-pink to lavender flowers grow in loose, nodding, rounded clusters.

Hardiness Zone 3a–7b

Bloom Period Summer

Growing Conditions Performs best in full sun to light shade and average-moisture, well-drained soils.

Nodding Onion is an easy-to-grow, low-maintenance native bulb. Its grassy, onion-scented foliage and distinctive pendulous blooms add beauty and soft texture to any landscape. The colorful blooms are particularly attractive to bees. Easy to establish, the delicate-looking plants are highly adaptable to soil conditions, and while drought tolerant, they thrive with extra moisture. Nodding Onion is a superb addition to cottage or rock gardens, in perennial beds, or for naturalizing in larger meadows or open woods and margins. This charming species is especially showy when planted in larger masses or drifts. Plants spread slowly by self-seed or bulb offshoots and can be easily cultivated by transplanting bulblets. The pungent odor and flavor of the plant parts tend to dissuade unwanted herbivory by browsing mammals, including deer and rabbits.

Attracts bees and occasionally butterflies.

Ohio Buckeye

Scientific Name *Aesculus glabra*

Family Sapindaceae

Plant Characteristics Deciduous tree up to 40 feet tall or more; large, coarse, palm-shaped, dark-green compound leaves have 5–7 elliptical leaflets with finely serrated margins; pale-yellow, tubular flowers grow in elongated, upright, terminal clusters.

Hardiness Zone 3a–7b

Bloom Period Spring

Growing Conditions Prefers full sun and moist, organically rich, well-drained soils.

A distinctive native tree of moist habitats, Ohio Buckeye is commonly found in mesic woodlands and along rivers and streams. It has an attractive, rounded growth habit; spreading branches; and large leaves, making it an ideal specimen or shade tree. It is also a great addition to any woodland garden. In spring, it produces showy, upright, nearly-foot-long clusters of tubular flowers that brighten the early-season landscape. The flowers are readily visited by Ruby-Throated Hummingbirds and various native bee species. Robust, rounded, spiky seed capsules develop later in summer; each contains one or more shiny, dark-brown seeds with a characteristic light-brown spot, or "eye," which is the origin of the species' common name. The raw seeds are poisonous to humans, livestock, and most wildlife. As summer wanes, Ohio Buckeye showcases reliable and early fall color, in hues of brilliant gold and orange. Several commercial cultivars are available.

Attracts bees and hummingbirds.

Pale Indian Plantain

Scientific Name *Arnoglossum atriplicifolium*

Family Asteraceae

Plant Characteristics Upright, herbaceous perennial up to 8 feet tall (or slightly taller); large, fan-shaped, green basal leaves have shallow lobes and undulating margins; terminal, flat-topped, branched clusters of small, white, tubular flowers are borne on robust, leafy stalks.

USDA Hardiness Zones 3b–7b

Bloom Period Midsummer–early fall

Growing Conditions Full sun and average to dry, well-drained soils.

Pale Indian Plantain is a striking wildflower of mesic woodlands; forest edges, slopes, and openings; and thickets and adjacent open areas in the southern portion of the region. Plants feature a base rosette of impressively large, leathery, and coarsely cleft leaves that can measure nearly 1 foot across. Late in the summer, the plants produce robust, leafy, flowering stalks that can reach 9 feet in height and tower over any adjacent vegetation. Sturdy, many-branched, flat clusters of tiny, creamy-white flowers bloom at the top. While not especially colorful, the resulting display is nonetheless quite eye-catching. Plants are relatively easy to grow and thrive with extra moisture, but they're not well suited for small garden spaces. Pale Indian Plantain can be used as a back-of-the-border specimen, but it's probably best incorporated into larger, more native landscapes.

Attracts bees, wasps, flies, and other insect pollinators.

Pickerelweed

Scientific Name *Pontederia cordata*

Family Pontederiaceae

Plant Characteristics Emergent aquatic or semiaquatic perennial up to 3 feet tall; large, smooth, somewhat waxy-looking, arrowhead-shaped basal leaves grow on long stalks; dense, elongated spikes of tubular, lobed, deep-violet-blue flowers are borne on stout, sheathed stems; the upper lobe has two yellow spots ringed in white.

USDA Hardiness Zones 3a–7b

Bloom Period Summer–early fall

Growing Conditions Performs best in full sun and shallow water or consistently waterlogged soils.

A true wetland plant, Pickerelweed typically grows in still, shallow water. The large, shiny leaves arise from submerged root stock and extend well above the water line. In a garden setting, it can tolerate soggy soil during drought conditions, but it should never be allowed to dry out. Plants spread by rhizomes and can readily form extensive colonies. The striking, almost-electric-blue flower spikes draw in a wide assortment of butterflies, bees, and other insects and are particularly eye-catching en masse. While individual flowers are short-lived, larger colonies can produce blooms for an extended time. This unique plant is a colorful and distinctive addition to small water gardens, including container gardens, as well as pond margins and larger wetland landscapes.

Attracts butterflies, bees, and other insect pollinators, as well as hummingbirds.

Purple Coneflower

Scientific Name *Echinacea purpurea*

Family Asteraceae

Plant Characteristics Stout, upright, herbaceous perennial up to 4 feet tall; coarse, oval to lance-shaped, green leaves get smaller up the hairy, purplish-green stems; large, daisylike flowers with pink to lavender, somewhat drooping rays surround a raised, spiny, brownish center.

Hardiness Zone 3a–7b

Bloom Period Summer–early fall

Growing Conditions Full sun and average to dry, well-drained soils. Although tolerant of poor soils and drought once established, richer garden soils and consistent moisture will enhance overall growth and flower production.

This showy wildflower is an absolute must for any butterfly or pollinator garden. The stout, upright plants are well suited for everything from containers and small garden spaces to larger perennial borders or naturalized meadows. Purple Coneflower is easy to grow and quite adaptable, tolerating a range of soil types. A long-blooming perennial, it produces a profuse show of colorful flowers that often lasts into early autumn. The domed, spiny centers provide a sturdy landing platform for butterflies and other pollinators, along with easy access to copious floral resources. It also makes a lovely cut flower. Purple Coneflower is widely available commercially, and numerous striking cultivars exist in various colors. Regular deadheading will encourage reblooming. The spent flower heads offer desirable resources of seed for hungry songbirds. Plants are easily propagated by seed or root division.

Attracts hummingbirds, butterflies, bees, and many other insect pollinators. Seeds are fed upon by songbirds.

Queen of the Prairie

Scientific Name *Filipendula rubra*

Family Rosaceae

Plant Characteristics Tall, upright, herbaceous perennial up to 6 feet tall or more; large, bright-green, deeply cut and serrated, palmlike leaves become smaller up the plant; dense, branched clusters of small, fuzzy-looking pink flowers perch atop sturdy stems.

Hardiness Zone 3a–7b

Bloom Period Summer

Growing Conditions Full sun and moist to wet, organically rich, well-drained soils.

Well named, this stately and unique perennial is a stunner in the landscape. Its large, fuzzy-looking, branched clusters of light-pink flowers, somewhat reminiscent of Astilbe, rise above much of the surrounding vegetation on tall, stout, and somewhat snaking stems. They bloom from the bottom up and, despite their showy appearance, offer no nectar. They do, however, provide ample pollen as a reward to bees and pollen-seeking insects. Even when not in flower, the bright, highly dissected leaves are quite ornamental. Plants thrive in wet locations but adapt well to organically rich garden soils, so long as regular irrigation is provided. Queen of the Prairie readily spreads by underground rhizomes to form colonies and is thus an excellent species for naturalizing in larger landscapes. It is particularly eye-catching en masse but can overwhelm smaller garden spaces.

Highly attractive to bees.

Roughleaf Dogwood

Scientific Name *Cornus drummondii*

Family Cornaceae

Plant Characteristics Large, deciduous shrub up to 15 feet tall or slightly more; large, oval, green leaves; flat, terminal clusters of creamy-yellow flowers.

USDA Hardiness Zones 5a–7b

Bloom Period Late spring–early summer

Growing Conditions Prefers full sun and moist, well-drained soils.

This native is an exceptional wildlife-attracting shrub. Named for the upper leaf surfaces, which are rough to the touch, it is fast-growing and spreads readily by underground rhizomes to form extensive colonies. A moisture-loving plant, Roughleaf Dogwood is ideal for less formal spaces in the landscape, such as naturalizing along woodland or wetland borders, or other moist to wet sites. The early-season flowers attract a bounty of pollinating insects. They are replaced by showy white berries that contrast with dark-green leaves, which eventually turn a rich crimson in fall. The overall display is highly ornamental. The fleshy fruits are a favorite of songbirds. The species is quite similar in appearance to the more widespread and abundant Gray Dogwood (*Cornus racemosa*), which tends to be shorter in stature.

Attracts butterflies, bees, flies, and other pollinators; serves as a larval host for the Spring Azure Butterfly (Celastrina ladon); birds eat the berries.

Showy Goldenrod

Scientific Name *Solidago speciosa*

Family Asteraceae

Plant Characteristics Upright, clump-forming herbaceous perennial up to 5 feet tall; long, stiff, lance-shaped to oblong green leaves occupy unbranched, green to reddish stems; small, yellow flowers form narrow, elongated, club-shaped, densely packed clusters.

Hardiness Zone 3a–7b

Bloom Period Late summer–fall

Growing Conditions Performs best in full sun and average to dry, well-drained soils.

Ideally named, Showy Goldenrod is one of the most striking members of this diverse genus. It is an unbranched wildflower that expands into sizable multistemmed clumps over time. Plants spread by underground rhizomes, making it ideal for naturalizing in larger open landscapes. It can become a bit aggressive under ideal growing conditions. A durable and easy-to-grow perennial, it is tolerant of poor soils and dry conditions, but it thrives in regular garden soils, requiring little care and adding ornamental value to any perennial border, wildlife garden, or cottage garden. In fact, with increased organic material and moisture, plants have a tendency to produce rapid but weak growth that often requires staking. The elongated, plumelike inflorescences are distinctive and tend to bloom slightly later than those of many other goldenrods. As a result, they provide a wealth of important late-season floral resources for foraging pollinators. After blooming, plants produce copious small, brown, elliptical seeds covered with light, fuzzy hairs to aid with wind dispersal.

Attracts butterflies, bees, beetles, and other insect pollinators and beneficial insects; various songbirds eat the seeds.

Showy Tick Trefoil

Scientific Name *Desmodium canadense*

Family Fabaceae

Plant Characteristics Upright, herbaceous perennial up to 5 feet tall; compound, hairy, gray-green leaves, each with 3 oblong leaflets that are rounded at the tips, on hairy stems; elongated, dense, terminal, spikelike clusters of large, light-pink to rose, pealike flowers.

USDA Hardiness Zones 3a–7b

Bloom Period Summer–early fall

Growing Conditions Full sun and average to moist, organically rich, well-drained soils.

Aptly named, this tall, somewhat sprawling wildflower is arguably one of the most attractive members of a notably weedy genus. It, like most other legumes, fixes atmospheric nitrogen, thereby improving soil health. Plants are easily grown and very drought tolerant once established. Best used in wildlife gardens, moist meadows, prairies, and other natural landscapes. Grouping plants together provides a highly conspicuous and appealing display. It also helps support the upright growth of plants that often have a tendency to flop somewhat. The dense clusters of handsome pink blooms are especially attractive to bees. After flowering, plants produce numerous flat, segmented seedpods, which are densely covered in fine, hooked hairs that readily cling to passing organisms to aid dispersal. Unfortunately, the pods can also stick to clothing and be a minor nuisance.

Attracts bees and other insect pollinators; serves as a larval host for Eastern Tailed-Blue (Everes comyntas), *Gray Hairstreak* (Strymon melinus), *Southern Cloudywing* (Thorybes bathyllus), *and Northern Cloudywing* (Thorybes pylades) *Butterflies.*

Smooth Blue Aster

Scientific Name *Symphyotrichum laeve*

Family Asteraceae

Plant Characteristics Upright, herbaceous, clump-forming perennial up to 4 feet tall; smooth, lanced-shaped, clasping, bright-green to somewhat gray-green leaves occupy mostly unbranched stems; terminal branched clusters of pale lavender-blue, daisylike flowers have bright-yellow centers.

USDA Hardiness Zones 3a–7b

Bloom Period Early to late fall

Growing Conditions Full sun and average to dry, moderately fertile, well-drained soils.

This late-season wildflower is yet another enchanting aster worthy of adding to your plantscape. It is named for its bright, clasping foliage that is noticeably smooth to the touch. Very easy to cultivate, Smooth Blue Aster tolerates a wide range of soils and moisture conditions, and it does not readily spread. It thrives in full sun and average soils and is quite drought tolerant once established. As fall approaches, the plants produce abundant airy clusters of lovely pale-blue flowers that are a late-season pollinator favorite. Great for mass-planting in meadows or as an eye-catching addition to any perennial border or cottage garden. Smooth Blue Aster is particularly showy combined with other color-ful fall-blooming perennials.

Attracts butterflies, bees, and other insect pollinators. Serves as a larval host for the Pearl Crescent Butterfly (Phyciodes tharos); various songbirds and small mammals consume the seeds.

Spotted Joe Pye Weed

Scientific Name *Eutrochium maculatum*

Family Asteraceae

Plant Characteristics Upright, herbaceous perennial up to 6 feet tall or more; highly textured, lance-shaped, green leaves occur in whorls spaced out along a stout, purplish stem; terminal, spreading, and somewhat flattened clusters of fuzzy pinkish flowers.

Hardiness Zone 3b–7b

Bloom Period Midsummer–early fall

Growing Conditions Full sun and moist to wet, organically rich soils.

Spotted Joe Pye Weed is a widespread and statuesque wetland perennial. (*Spotted* refers to the noticeably rosy stem, which is dotted with darker purple spots.) At home in fens, marshes, and wet meadows, it's wonderful for naturalizing or in sunny, soggy, and often waterlogged landscape sites such as rain gardens. It adapts to rich garden soils with regular irrigation. It is particularly attractive planted both en masse and in combination with other showy wetland perennials such as Common Boneset (page 151), Blue Vervain (page 45), and Culver's Root (page 57), to name a few. The multistemmed plants expand into sizable clumps with age, providing elements of height as well as texture. The large, fuzzy flower heads are quite impressive and an absolute magnet for bees, butterflies, and other insect pollinators. Spotted Joe Pye Weed spreads by underground rhizomes and can form larger colonies over time. A few commercial cultivars are available.

Attracts butterflies, bees, and many other insect pollinators.

Stiff Goldenrod

Scientific Name *Oligoneuron rigidum*

Family Asteraceae

Plant Characteristics Upright, herbaceous perennial up to 5 feet tall; long, oblong, gray-green, semievergreen basal leaves; tall, flat-topped, branching clusters of small, densely packed, yellow flowers are borne on stout, leafy stems.

Hardiness Zone 3a–7b

Bloom Period Late summer–fall

Growing Conditions Performs best in full sun and average, well-drained soils.

This native is yet another distinctive fall perennial that provides both beauty and high-quality floral resources for the landscape. Previously part of the genus *Solidago*, Stiff Goldenrod is easy to cultivate and not overly particular about soil type or condition, provided that the soil is well drained. The durable plants are quite tolerant of poor soils and drought. The species boasts characteristically large, rough basal leaves that are covered in small, white hairs, giving the vegetation an overall gray-green appearance. These basal leaves typically remain somewhat green over the winter. In later summer, plants send up tall, leafy stalks that support branched, flat clusters of golden blooms, lasting well into fall. The bountiful resources are a magnet to Monarch Butterflies and other insect pollinators. Stiff Goldenrod can be a bit weedy, spreading by both seed and underground rhizomes, so it may not be the best choice for smaller garden settings. It is, however, wonderful for naturalizing in meadows; savannas; and other open, sunny areas. The resulting show is quite appealing, particularly en masse.

Attracts butterflies, bees, wasps, and many other insect pollinators.

Swamp Rosemallow

Scientific Name *Hibiscus moscheutos*

Family Malvaceae

Plant Characteristics Upright, herbaceous perennial up to 7 feet tall; large, oval to broadly lance-shaped, green to gray-green leaves with serrated margins are borne on sturdy green stems; large, saucer-shaped, pink to white flowers with crimson centers are borne from the upper leaf axils.

USDA Hardiness Zones 5a–7b

Bloom Period Summer–early fall

Growing Conditions Full sun and fertile, moist to wet soils.

This stately, moisture-loving wildflower is at home in wetlands and along stream or pond margins in more-southern portions of the region. While it thrives in wet, organically rich soils, it is adaptable to more-traditional garden settings with regular irrigation. Plants produce multiple sturdy stems and can form sizable shrubby clumps over time. Swamp Rosemallow is a great addition to rain gardens and other perpetually soggy, sunny sites in the landscape; it also makes an attractive addition to the back of a perennial border. The plants are particularly impressive when planted in groups. The large leaves provide an excellent backdrop for the stunning flowers, which have five overlapping, pink to creamy-white petals with a crimson center and a prominent central staminal column. Each flower's distinctively dark center is the inspiration for the species' other common name, Crimsoneyed Rosemallow. Although they are short-lived, the enormous blooms can measure more than 6 inches across. Several commercial cultivars are available.

Attracts butterflies, bees, and other insect pollinators, as well as hummingbirds.

Tall Cinquefoil

Scientific Name *Drymocallis arguta*

Family Rosaceae

Plant Characteristics Upright, herbaceous perennial up to 3 feet tall; pale-green leaves are compound, hairy, and mostly basal; individual leaflets are oval, with highly serrated margins and a rounded tip; limited stem leaves; tight clusters of white, 5-petaled flowers have yellow anthers and green, leafy bracts on terminally branched, hairy stems.

Hardiness Zone 3a–7b

Bloom Period Summer–early fall

Growing Conditions Performs best in full sun to partial shade and average to dry, well-drained soils.

Previously in the genus Potentilla, this is a distinctive wildflower of fields, savannas, and woodland borders. All parts of the plant are densely covered in fine, whitish hairs that give it an overall light-green to gray-green appearance. Sturdy, erect stems shoot up in summer to showcase densely packed clusters of yellow-centered, creamy-white blooms that superficially resemble white buttercups. While the flowers are not overly attractive to pollinators, many small native bees and flower-loving flies are frequent visitors. Tall Cinquefoil is not overly fussy about soil type or conditions, provided that the soil is well drained. Established plants are quite drought tolerant, experience few pest problems, and require little maintenance. Tall Cinquefoil is a showy and highly underutilized addition to sunny meadows, dry woodland edges, or perennial beds and borders; it also makes a good addition to a rock garden.

Attracts small, native, short-tonged bees and syrphid (flower) flies.

Trumpet Honeysuckle

Scientific Name *Lonicera sempervirens*

Family Caprifoliaceae

Plant Characteristics Deciduous, twining vine up to 15 feet in length; smooth, oval leaves are bluish green, with some often fused around the stem higher up on the plant; loose clusters of long, tubular, coral-red flowers have a yellow interior.

USDA Hardiness Zones 4a–7b

Bloom Period Summer–early fall

Growing Conditions Full sun and organically rich, average to moist, well-drained soils.

This delightful species is arguably one of our most attractive native vines. A vigorous grower with a slender, twining habit, it's perfect for sunny fencerows, arbors, and trellises. While Trumpet Honeysuckle will tolerate some shade, flower production often dips or stops in shadier parts of the landscape. Plants boast attractive, shiny foliage and an abundance of flashy blooms that are tubular and somewhat pendulous. The prominent coral-colored flowers have no fragrance but are an absolute magnet for Ruby-Throated Hummingbirds; sphinx moths and larger butterflies and bees will also visit the blooms. Once flowering is complete, the vine produces small, glossy red berries that are readily fed upon by songbirds. Also called Coral Honeysuckle, it is widely available at native plant nurseries and many specialty garden centers. Several commercial cultivars vary in flower color.

Attracts hummingbirds, sphinx moths, and occasionally some larger butterflies; serves as a larval host for Snowberry Clearwing (Hemaris diffinis) *and Hummingbird Clearwing* (Hemaris thysbe) *moths; songbirds readily consume the fruit.*

Virginia Mountainmint

Scientific Name *Pycnanthemum virginianum*

Family Lamiaceae

Plant Characteristics Upright, branching, herbaceous perennial up to 3 feet tall; narrow, lance-shaped to almost linear, grasslike, light-green leaves grow on square, green to reddish-green stems; small, flattened, terminal clusters of small, lobed, tubular flowers are either solid white or white with purple spots.

Hardiness Zone 3b–7b

Bloom Period Midsummer–early fall

Growing Conditions Full sun and average to moist, well-drained soils.

This distinctive wildflower is an exceptional pollinator magnet. The compact, multibranched plants have an overall bushy appearance and green, pleasingly minty-scented foliage. Starting in midsummer and often continuing until early autumn, Virginia Mountainmint produces dense, terminal clusters of tiny, tubular, pure-white or purple-spotted white flowers. The resulting profusion of floral resources strongly lures a wide assortment of insects and adds an almost frosty appearance to the landscape, especially if planted en masse. Plants are easy to grow and not overly fussy about soil type or condition. While it thrives in moist, brightly lit locations, it adapts quite well to most garden soils and can even tolerate drought once established. Plants expand to form small colonies over time, spreading readily by underground rhizomes. Virginia Mountainmint's low maintenance, beauty, long blooming period, and undeniable insect attraction make it a top choice for pollinator and wildlife gardens or for naturalizing in larger landscapes.

Attracts butterflies, bees, wasps, and many other insect pollinators.

Western Pearly Everlasting

Scientific Name *Anaphalis margaritacea*

Family Asteraceae

Plant Characteristics Upright, clump-forming, herbaceous perennial up to 3 feet tall; leaves are narrow, pointed, gray-green; papery white bracts surround flat-topped, terminal clusters of small, yellowish flowers.

Hardiness Zone 3a–7b

Bloom Period Summer–fall

Growing Conditions Performs best in full sun and average-moisture, sandy to rocky, well-drained soils.

A durable species of dry, poor soils in forest clearings, meadows, and waste areas, Western Pearly Everlasting is often found in larger colonies. The stems and leaves are densely covered in woolly white hairs, resulting in an overall silvery to grayish appearance. While the plants are somewhat raggedy looking in general, the late-season flowers are certainly worth the wait. The showy, papery white bracts look like petals, completely surrounding and overshadowing the actual flowers, which are tiny and yellow. Numerous insect pollinators frequent the distinctive blooms. The species is dioecious, with male and female flowers growing on different plants. Aptly named, the terminal clusters of Western Pearly Everlasting dry and remain on the plant long after flowering is complete, making it an excellent addition to dried arrangements. Easy to grow and drought tolerant, it requires little maintenance once established.

Attracts butterflies, bees, and other insect pollinators; larval host for American Lady (Vanessa virginiensis) *and Painted Lady* (Vanessa cardui) *Butterflies.*

Whorled Milkweed

Scientific Name *Asclepias verticillata*

Family Apocynaceae

Plant Characteristics Upright, herbaceous perennial up to 2½ feet in height or slightly taller; long, linear, needlelike, green leaves in whorls around smooth, unbranched stems; loose axillary clusters of small, greenish-white flowers.

Hardiness Zone 4a–7b

Bloom Period Summer–early fall

Growing Conditions Full sun and average to dry, well-drained soils.

This unique perennial is typically found in dry, open woodlands, grasslands, and rocky forests, as well as in dry fields and along roadsides and power easements. The airy, unbranched plants feature numerous needlelike leaves and are somewhat reminiscent of a bottlebrush in appearance; as a result, Whorled Milkweed can easily be overlooked among the surrounding herbs and grasses. Plants readily spread by rhizomes to form fairly dense colonies over time, but they seldom become overly weedy. The delicate clusters of greenish-white flowers, occasionally tinged with purple, are less showy than those of many other milkweed species, but they still provide an attractive show, as well as floral resources for a range of insect visitors. After flowering, plants produce elongated, narrow, upward-pointing seedpods that taper toward the tips. Plants are easy to grow from seed and require little care once established, being tolerant of poor soils and drought. Whorled Milkweed is a great choice for a perennial border, wildflower meadow, or dry woodland garden.

Attracts butterflies, bees, and many other insect pollinators; serves as a larval food plant for the Monarch Butterfly (Danaus plexippus).

Winged Lythrum

Scientific Name *Lythrum alatum*

Family Lythraceae

Plant Characteristics Upright, herbaceous perennial up to 4 feet tall; smooth, green, lance-shaped to elliptical leaves have smooth margins; leaves become smaller up the noticeably 4-sided, winged stem; tubular, lavender flowers, each with 6 spreading lobes, grow in narrow, spikelike clusters; flowers are produced in leaf axils.

USDA Hardiness Zones 3b–7b

Bloom Period Summer–early fall

Growing Conditions Full sun and organically rich, moist to wet soils.

Winged Lythrum is a lovely wildflower of wetlands, moist meadows, and wet ditches. It is named for the distinctive raised, longitudinal ridges, or "wings," along its stems. Plants produce elongated, narrow flower clusters with one to several lavender-colored blooms along each stalk. The star-shaped flowers are quite attractive to various insects ranging from large butterflies to small native bees. Requiring fertile soil and regular moisture, it makes a showy addition to rain gardens; pond, stream, or other wetland margins; or any low, perpetually soggy sites in the landscape. Also called Winged Loosestrife, Winged Lythrum may occasionally be confused with the highly invasive Purple Loosestrife, which has rampaged through wetland habitats and displaced native vegetation in the process.

Attracts butterflies, bees, and flies.

White Turtlehead

Pink Swamp Milkweed

Wild Bergamot

Full Sun to Partial Shade

Eastern Redbud

Buttonbush

Partridge Pea

Red Maple

From Northern Spicebush (page 179) to Scarlet Beebalm (page 199), some pollinator- or wildlife-friendly favorites are somewhat adaptive when it comes to light level, performing well in either full sun or partial shade. These plants can tolerate 3–6 hours of direct sunlight per day but will often bloom more profusely with extended, but not direct, sunlight. Such plants are often good choices for open woodlands, forest margins, or other less-than-full-sun locations in the landscape.

Golden Alexanders

Blue Mistflower

Cardinal Flower

Allegheny Serviceberry

Scientific Name *Amelanchier laevis*

Family Rosaceae

Plant Characteristics Large, deciduous shrub or small tree up to 30 feet tall or more; oval, green leaves have finely serrated margins and reddish-brown branches; terminal, somewhat drooping clusters of fragrant, white, 5-petaled flowers; round, berrylike, purple-black fruit.

USDA Hardiness Zones 4a–7b

Bloom Period Midspring

Growing Conditions Performs best in full sun to partial shade and moist, organically rich, well-drained soils.

Allegheny Serviceberry is a wonderful woodland native that offers both year-round landscape interest and outstanding wildlife value. Typically grown as large shrubs or small, often multitrunked trees, plants have an airy and architecturally graceful branching habit that results in a generally rounded crown. Abundant clusters of bright-white flowers festoon the bare branches in spring, lending an early-season pop of cheer to the landscape. The short-lived but copious blooms attract an array of different pollinating insects. The flowers are replaced by small, round, red, berrylike fruits that turn a rich dark purple by early summer, when they mature; the resulting bounty is a favorite of many songbirds and small mammals. The show continues late into the season as the leaves turn brilliant shades of yellow to reddish orange, affording an exceptional autumnal display. Whether planted as a specimen, clustered together in small groupings, or naturalized in an open woodland or along a forest border, Allegheny Serviceberry is an exceptional addition to the landscape.

Attracts butterflies, bees, and other insect pollinators; birds eat the berries.

Alternateleaf Dogwood

Scientific Name *Cornus alternifolia*

Family Cornaceae

Plant Characteristics Large, deciduous shrub to 25 feet tall (or slightly taller); large, oval, prominently veined, green leaves on green, brown, or purplish stems; flat clusters of fragrant, creamy-yellow flowers.

USDA Hardiness Zones 3a–7b

Bloom Period Late spring–early summer

Growing Conditions Full sun to partial shade and moist, organically rich, well-drained soils.

This native shrub of understories and forest borders is prized for its high ornamental value. As its name suggests, plants boast large, shiny, green leaves that are alternately arranged. Also called Pagoda Dogwood, it has distinctive tiered, horizontal branching that creates a lovely, airy, spreading architecture. In late spring, plants produce an abundance of broad, fuzzy-looking, creamy-yellow flower clusters that seem to almost hover over the leafy branches. The flowers are soon replaced by small, rounded, reddish-purple fruits that mature to a blackish blue by late summer. The approaching autumn transforms the green leaves to handsome shades of red or magenta, electrifying the late-season landscape. Alternateleaf Dogwood is relatively easy to grow and quite adaptable, tolerating a range of soil and light conditions. It makes a superb specimen, showy border or foundation plant, privacy screen, or woodland-garden addition.

Attracts butterflies, bees, wasps, flies, and other pollinators; serves as a larval host plant for the Spring Azure Butterfly (Celastrina ladon); birds and small mammals eat the fruit; provides cover and nesting sites for songbirds.

American Black Elderberry

Scientific Name *Sambucus nigra* ssp. *canadensis*

Family Caprifoliaceae

Plant Characteristics Upright, deciduous shrub up to 10 feet tall or more; compound, bright- to dark-green leaves are borne on gray-brown branches; individual leaflets are elliptical to lance-shaped, with finely serrated margins; small, creamy-white flowers grow in broad, flat to somewhat dome-shaped clusters.

USDA Hardiness Zones 3a–7b

Bloom Period Late spring–midsummer

Growing Conditions Full sun to partial shade and moist, organically rich soils.

Also called Common Elderberry or American Elder, this is a common and widespread shrub throughout the region. A fast-growing and pioneer species, it may be encountered in a wide range of moist habitats, from stream and woodland margins to wet ditches and shrubby rights-of-way. Plants feature handsome green foliage and broad, somewhat lacy clusters of small, whitish flowers. The resulting pleasingly fragrant blooms attract a wide range of insects. As summer progresses, the robust shrubs are adorned with clusters of dark, purplish-black, berrylike fruits that are readily consumed by birds and other wildlife. American Black Elderberry spreads by underground rhizomes and can quickly form larger thickets; while this requires some regular maintenance in a garden setting, it is ideal for naturalizing along ponds, streams, or other moist sites in the landscape.

Attracts butterflies, bees, flies, beetles, and other pollinators. The fruit is eaten by songbirds and small mammals; the hollow branches provide nesting sites for many native bee species.

Black Cherry

Scientific Name *Prunus serotina*

Family Rosaceae

Plant Characteristics Deciduous tree up to 80 feet tall or more; elliptical, bright-green leaves have serrated margins; small, white, semifragrant, 5-petaled flowers with yellowish centers grow in elongated, pendulous clusters.

USDA Hardiness Zones 3a–7b

Bloom Period Spring

Growing Conditions Prefers full sun to partial shade and average-moisture, well-drained soils.

When it comes to attracting wildlife, Black Cherry is an exceptional species that is often overlooked for its ornamental value. Trees boast appealingly smooth, shiny, green leaves; dark, flaky bark; and an overall pyramidal form. In spring, it produces a profusion of elongated, showy flower clusters, each up to 6 inches or longer. The copious blooms attract bees, flies, and other insect pollinators. The flowers are quickly replaced by clusters of small, round, red fruits that mature to a purplish black; these are a favorite food of many hungry songbirds. Extremely fast-growing and easy to cultivate, plants can be somewhat weedy and aggressive, with seeds being readily spread by birds. Fallen berries are somewhat messy and can leave stains on decks, driveways, or nearby structures. That said, the many wildlife benefits of Black Cherry greatly outweigh these minor drawbacks, especially when used in more-natural settings.

Attracts butterflies, bees, flies, and other pollinators. Serves as a larval host for Eastern Tiger Swallowtail (Papilio glaucus)*, Red-Spotted Purple* (Limenitis arthemis astyanax)*, Coral Hairstreak* (Satyrium titus)*, and occasionally Summer Azure* (Celastrina neglecta) *Butterflies; the fruit is eaten by songbirds, game birds, and small mammals.*

Blue Mistflower

Scientific Name *Conoclinium coelestinum*

Family Asteraceae

Plant Characteristics Compact, branching, herbaceous perennial 2½ feet tall; triangular, prominently veined, green leaves have toothed margins; flat-topped clusters of small, tubular, light-blue to purplish-blue flowers sit atop upright, purplish-green stalks.

USDA Hardiness Zones 5b–7b

Bloom Period Summer–fall

Growing Conditions Performs best in full sun to partial shade and organically rich, moist soils.

This distinctive wildflower is also called Hardy Ageratum because of its resemblance to the common garden annual. It thrives in perpetually moist locations but is also adaptable to garden settings as long as the soil is rich with organic material and regularly irrigated. Established plants can tolerate some drought, especially in partially shaded areas, but they perform poorly without consistent moisture. A somewhat weedy plant for small spaces, Blue Mistflower spreads aggressively by underground rhizomes or seed, often forming dense stands; this growth habit makes it an excellent choice for naturalizing in wetland gardens, open woodlands, or along streams or ponds. A prolific bloomer, Blue Mistflower produce a profusion of dense, powdery-blue flower clusters that are highly enticing to a wide range of insect pollinators.

Attracts butterflies, bees, and other insect pollinators.

Blue Wild Indigo

Scientific Name *Baptisia australis*

Family Fabaceae

Plant Characteristics Clump-forming, upright, herbaceous perennial up to 5 feet tall; green to somewhat bluish-green, cloverlike leaves on smooth, stout stems; elongated spikes of light- to dark-blue, pealike flowers.

USDA Hardiness Zones 3a–7b

Bloom Period Late spring–midsummer

Growing Conditions Full sun to partial shade and dry to somewhat moist, well-drained soils. Adapts well to a variety of garden soils.

This bushy native is one of the most widely cultivated members of the genus *Baptisia* and a true garden favorite. Blue Wild Indigo has a relatively long bloom period and offers season-long interest. Although somewhat slow to establish, the plant expands over time into dense, somewhat spreading, multistemmed clumps that are often wider than they are tall. Highly attractive individually or planted in smaller groups, Blue Wild Indigo is easy to grow and durable, and it can be incorporated into more-formal perennial borders as well as wild, natural spaces. A dwarf variety is also available for smaller landscapes. The stately plants produce numerous long, upright spires of striking blue flowers that are readily visited by bumblebees. Later in the season, the vibrant flowers give way to inflated, dull-black seedpods for continued botanical interest and appeal.

Particularly attractive to bumblebees. Butterflies and hummingbirds occasionally visit the blooms; periodically used as a larval host by the Wild Indigo Duskywing (Erynnis baptisiae).

Bluebell Bellflower

Scientific Name *Campanula rotundifolia*

Family Campanulaceae

Plant Characteristics Upright, herbaceous perennial to 1½ feet tall; dark-green, heart-shaped basal leaves; slender stems bear linear, grass-like leaves; individual or loose clusters of bell-shaped, violet-colored flowers.

Hardiness Zone 3a–7b

Bloom Period Summer

Growing Conditions Full sun to partial shade and average to dry, well-drained soils.

Also called Harebell, this graceful perennial adds colorful splendor to the landscape. In early summer, plant bursts forth with characteristic nodding, bell-shaped flowers that are supported on sleek, treadlike stalks. The striking violet-colored blooms may continue to be sporadically produced throughout the summer, especially with regular deadheading; they are primarily visited by bees and some butterflies. Despite their delicate appearance, the compact plants regularly thrive in harsh soil conditions, are quite drought tolerant, and are easy to grow from seed. Bluebell Bellflower is an ideal choice for cottage or rock gardens or smaller perennial beds; it's also good for naturalizing in open woodlands, rocky slopes, or meadows. Grouping plants together provides the best visual impact.

Attracts butterflies and bees.

Brown-Eyed Susan

Scientific Name *Rudbeckia triloba*

Family Asteraceae

Plant Characteristics Upright, branched biennial or short-lived, herbaceous perennial up to 5 feet tall; coarse, somewhat hairy, lance-shaped to oval, entire to lobed, dark-green leaves; daisylike flowers have stubby, rounded, yellow rays surrounding a dark-brown to black center atop stiff, branched, reddish-brown stems.

USDA Hardiness Zones 3b–7b

Bloom Period Midsummer–midfall

Growing Conditions Performs best in full sun to partial shade and average to moist, organically rich, well-drained soils.

While this attractive wildflower thrives in organically rich, moist locations, it is highly adaptable to a variety of garden conditions and is relatively tolerant of heat, drought, and poorer soils. Established plants produce bushy, densely branched clumps that yield an impressive profusion of small, golden-yellow blooms, each with conspicuously dark centers. The resulting display can be quite spectacular and provides an abundance of floral resources to bees, butterflies, and a wide assortment of other insect pollinators. The regular deadheading of spent flowers promotes reblooming. Although short-lived, plants freely self-seed and can become a bit weedy, especially in small spaces. Showy en masse or individually, Brown-Eyed Susan is a welcome addition to any perennial border, but it is probably best used in a native meadow or planted along moist woodlands or wetland margins.

Attracts butterflies, bees, and other insect pollinators; various songbirds feed on the seeds.

Burningbush

Scientific Name *Euonymus atropurpureus*

Family Celastraceae

Plant Characteristics Large, deciduous shrub or small tree up to 20 feet tall (or taller); oval to elliptical, dark-green leaves have finely serrated margins; loose, axillary clusters of 4-petaled reddish-brown to purple flowers.

USDA Hardiness Zone 3a–7b

Bloom Period Late spring–early summer

Growing Conditions Full sun to partial shade and average to moist, organically rich, well-drained soils.

Also called American Wahoo, this is a distinctive native shrub of mesic woodlands, riverbanks, and adjacent partially shaded habitats. Plants produce unusual airy flower clusters along the branches in spring. The small individual blooms have spreading, oval, purplish petals that are somewhat reminiscent of carrion flowers. The resulting lobed seed capsules are pinkish red and pendulous, hanging off the branches by slender stalks. They mature in autumn and burst open to reveal small, shiny, rounded, red fruit. Accompanied by brilliant-red fall foliage that truly makes the plant appear ablaze, the resulting show is quite eye-catching. Burningbush thrives in light shade and fertile soils, but it can be somewhat short-lived. Although it has ornamental properties, it is probably best used in more-naturalistic settings such as a woodland garden or other perpetually moist sites in the landscape.

Attracts bees, flies, and beetles.

Buttonbush

Scientific Name *Cephalanthus occidentalis*

Family Rubiaceae

Plant Characteristics Deciduous shrub up to 12 feet or more in height; bright, shiny, elliptical, green leaves on often arching branches; dense, spherical clusters of tiny, white, tubular flowers on long stalks.

USDA Hardiness Zones 4b–7b

Bloom Period Summer

Growing Conditions Full sun to partial shade and moist to wet, organically rich soils.

A distinctive shrub of wetland habitats, Buttonbush thrives in consistently moist conditions and can withstand periodic inundation. Despite this preference, it adapts well to most organically rich garden soils that have regular irrigation. Plants have a lovely, arching form and are generally spread much wider than their overall height. They showcase attractive, glossy, green foliage and truly unique, round flower clusters, each about the size of a ping-pong ball. Every tiny flower displays a single white style that projects well beyond the petals and gives the overall cluster a characteristic pincushion-like appearance. The fragrant blooms draw in a wide assortment of insect pollinators. This species is outstandingly wildlife-friendly and a great addition to a rain garden, pollinator garden, or pond or stream margin; it's also good for naturalizing in wetter areas of the landscape. Several available cultivars have more-compact growth habits. *Note:* This plant is toxic if ingested.

Attracts butterflies, bees, and other insect pollinators, as well as hummingbirds. Swallowtails literally swarm the blossoms; numerous birds feed on the resulting seeds.

Canada Lily

Scientific Name *Lilium canadense*

Family Liliaceae

Plant Characteristics Upright, herbaceous perennial up to 4 feet tall or slightly more; smooth, narrow, elliptical, green leaves grow in staggered whorls along a central, unbranched, green stem; 1 to many terminal, nodding, yellow-orange to red-orange, trumpet-shaped flowers are borne on long stalks, and each flower has 6 flaring, recurved stepals; a purple spotted throat; and long, protruding anthers.

USDA Hardiness Zones 3a–7b

Bloom Period Late spring–midsummer

Growing Conditions Full sun to partial shade and organically rich, moist, well-drained soils.

Canada Lily is a widespread wildflower of moist meadows; wet, forested slopes; and rich, deciduous woodlands. When in full bloom, the tall plants produce a varying number of showy, pendulous blooms, resulting in a highly ornamental display that is simply exquisite, especially when planted in groupings. The blooms are particularly attractive to larger butterflies, particularly various swallowtails, which readily maneuver into the flower from below. Thriving in organically rich soils with regular moisture, Canada Lily is a wonderful addition to perennial borders and rain and cottage gardens, or for naturalizing in larger, open to semiopen landscapes. The added height is perfect for the back of a border and for adding some structure to smaller garden spaces. Well-established plants can tolerate temporary drought.

Highly attractive to butterflies, sphinx moths, and hummingbirds.

Canada Milkvetch

Scientific Name *Astragalus canadensis*

Family Fabaceae

Plant Characteristics Upright to sprawling perennial up to 3 feet tall; compound, fernlike, green leaves have many narrow, oblong leaflets; elongated axillary spikelike clusters of tubular, pealike, cream to light-greenish-yellow flowers.

USDA Hardiness Zones 3a–7b

Bloom Period Summer

Growing Conditions Full sun to partial shade and average to moist, well-drained soils.

Canada Milkvetch is an attractive and highly useful landscape plant. The plant's long taproot helps stabilize the soil and prevent erosion, and like other legumes, it fixes atmospheric nitrogen. An adaptable wildflower, it is often encountered in a variety of habitats, from glades and savannas to old fields and along woodland margins. It is an equally worthy garden plant that is easy to grow with little fuss or maintenance. The abundant, lacy foliage adds a lovely, soft, and somewhat airy texture. Canada Milkvetch has a somewhat sprawling growth habit that benefits from neighboring plants holding it more erect. Starting in midsummer and continuing for over a month or so, plants are adorned with distinctive long, creamy flower clusters. The tubular blooms are replaced by equally showy pointed, oval seedpods that turn a dark blackish brown when mature. They persist well through the winter, adding another layer of interest to the often bleak late-season landscape.

Attracts bees (particularly bumblebees) and hummingbirds; seeds are consumed by game birds and small mammals.

Cardinal Flower

Scientific Name *Lobelia cardinalis*

Family Campanulaceae

Plant Characteristics Herbaceous perennial up to 5 feet tall; lance-shaped, dark-green leaves have toothed margins; terminal, spikelike clusters of lobed, tubular, bright-red flowers are borne on sturdy, upright stalks.

USDA Hardiness Zones 3a–7b

Bloom Period Summer–midfall

Growing Conditions Performs best in full sun to partial shade and organically rich, moist soils.

This stunning species is named for its vibrant, tubular, cardinal-red blossoms, which are a favorite of Ruby-Throated Hummingbirds. Some larger butterflies, such as swallowtails, also frequent the blossoms. A moisture-loving and clump-forming perennial, Cardinal Flower is a showy addition to regularly soggy sites; rain or wetland gardens; or pond and stream borders, where it prospers in full sun to filtered shade. It is particularly stunning when planted in numbers, and it is adaptable to more-traditional perennial garden settings with fertile, highly organic soils as long as regular irrigation is provided. Cardinal Flower is intolerant of drought, and sites where it is planted should not be allowed to dry out. Plants are short-lived and typically persist for only a few years, but they freely self-seed as well as reproduce via basal offshoots. The resulting seedlings and young plants grow quickly. Several commercial cultivars are available that vary in flower and foliage color.

Attracts hummingbirds and butterflies.

Chokecherry

Scientific Name *Prunus virginiana*

Family Rosaceae

Plant Characteristics Large, deciduous shrub or small tree up to 25 feet or more in height; broadly elliptical to oval, green leaves have serrated margins on spreading branches; elongated, dense clusters of somewhat fragrant, 5-petaled, small, white flowers with yellowish centers.

USDA Hardiness Zones 2a–7b

Bloom Period Spring–early summer

Growing Conditions Performs best in full sun to partial shade and average, well-drained soils.

Like other *Prunus* species, Chokecherry is an exceptional wildlife-attracting native. Shorter in stature than its close relatives, plants feature dense, ascending branches that grow in a rounded to somewhat irregular form. In spring, the branches are copiously adorned with dense, bottlebrush-shaped clusters of small, white, and fragrantly scented blooms that provide an abundance of early-season resources for many flower-visiting insects. The showy flowers are replaced by hanging clusters of dark-cherry-colored, berrylike fruit that is particularly appealing to birds. In early autumn, the green leaves turn lovely hues of yellow to peach. Chokecherry is fast-growing and easy to cultivate in a range of soil types and conditions. The plant spreads by suckering and can form thickets if not controlled. It nonetheless makes a good specimen, screen, or addition to sunny, more-naturalistic landscapes.

Attracts butterflies, bees, flies, and other pollinators. Serves as a larval host for Red-Spotted Purple (Limenitis arthemis astyanax), Coral Hairstreak (Satyrium titus), and Cherry Gall Azure (Celastrina serotina) Butterflies; the fruit is eaten by songbirds, game birds, and small mammals.

Common Boneset

Scientific Name *Eupatorium perfoliatum*

Family Asteraceae

Plant Characteristics Upright, clump-forming, herbaceous perennial up to 5 feet tall; highly textured, opposite, lance-shaped green to yellow-green leaves have serrated margins, the bases of which merge together around the central hairy stem; terminal, flat clusters of fuzzy, white flowers.

USDA Hardiness Zones 3a–7b

Bloom Period Summer–early fall

Growing Conditions Performs best in full sun to partial shade and moist to wet, organically rich soils.

This clump-forming wetland native boasts long, arching, green leaves that fuse together around a noticeably hairy stem; the conspicuous venation gives them a distinctive wrinkled appearance. Later in summer, plants produce handsome branched clusters of small, white flowers that give the entire flower head a somewhat fuzzy appearance. Although not overly showy, the blooms are readily visited by a wide range of insect pollinators. Common Boneset thrives in perpetually moist, organically rich soils and is a wonderful addition to a stream or pond margin, a soggy woodland border, an open wetland, or a rain garden. It can even withstand inundation for short periods of time. Plants spread by underground rhizomes to form larger colonies over time. Common Boneset is highly attractive when combined with other colorful, moisture-loving perennials, and it provides a great pop of white to the late-season landscape, in which yellow, pink, and purple colors often dominate.

Attracts butterflies, bees, and other insect pollinators.

Common Evening Primrose

Scientific Name *Oenothera biennis*

Family Onagraceae

Plant Characteristics Upright herbaceous biennial up to
6 feet tall (or slightly taller); elliptical to lance-shaped,
green to olive-green leaves with smooth or slightly
toothed margins on stout, red-tinted green stems;
terminal clusters of 4-petaled, light-yellow flowers.

USDA Hardiness Zones 4a–7b

Bloom Period Summer–early fall

Growing Conditions Full sun to partial shade and average to dry,
well-drained soils.

Common Evening Primrose is a widespread wildflower equally at
home in pristine natural habitats and disturbed sites. Plants start out
by forming thick basal rosettes before sending up multiple sturdy
and heavily leaved flowering stems in their second year. The resulting bushy, robust plants may reach the height of a basketball player
and can tower over adjacent herbaceous vegetation. The distinctive
yellow blooms open during the evening and close by early-morning
light, being pollinated predominantly by sphinx moths. This unique
trait is the inspiration behind the common name evening primrose.
Flowers give way to elongated capsules, which turn brown at maturity
and explode open to release copious amounts of small, dark seeds,
after which the plant dies. As a result, Common Evening Primrose is
ideal for naturalizing but also makes a unique addition to the back
of a perennial bed or pollinator garden. Plants are easy to cultivate,
adaptable, and quite tolerant of drought

*Attracts moths and bees; serves as the larval host for the White-
Lined Sphinx Moth (Hyles lineata); songbirds eat the seeds.*

Common Hackberry

Scientific Name *Celtis occidentalis*

Family Cannabaceae

Plant Characteristics Deciduous tree up to 60 feet or more in height; rough, broadly lance-shaped, green leaves have serrated margins; yellow-green flowers are small, inconspicuous.

USDA Hardiness Zones 2a–7b

Bloom Period Spring–early summer

Growing Conditions Full sun to partial shade and moist, organically rich, well-drained soils.

Common Hackberry is a high-wildlife-value addition to more-naturalistic landscapes. This widespread native tree features grayish bark and a broad crown with wide, arching branches, making it a sound landscape choice. These features make it a delightful shade tree, although regular pruning is often needed to shape and develop a strong branch structure. It is also a useful addition to any moist woodland site or along waterways. A relatively fast grower, it is tolerant of a range of conditions, including poorer soils and increased shade, but it thrives in moist sites. After spring flowering, trees produce edible, fleshy, purple-black, berrylike fruit that provides a wealth of food resources for a range of songbirds and small mammals. The copious fruit often lingers on trees well into early winter. The densely branched trees also offer good cover and nesting resources for birds.

Attracts butterflies and serves as a larval host for several species; songbirds and small mammals feed on the fruit.

Common Hoptree

Scientific Name *Ptelea trifoliata*

Family Rutaceae

Plant Characteristics Small deciduous tree up to 20 feet in height; compound shiny, bright-green aromatic leaves, each having three elliptical leaflets; dome-like terminal clusters of small, 4- to 5-petaled, greenish-white flowers.

USDA Hardiness Zones 3a–7b

Bloom Period Late spring–early summer

Growing Conditions Full sun to partial shade and average, well-drained soils.

This small but handsome tree often features several low, ascending, and often intertwining branches from the base, making it appear more like a shrub. Its ornamental growth habit, combined with a rounded crown, makes it a perfect accent plant for smaller landscapes. The glossy, green leaves have a strong citrus odor when crushed. The airy and fragrant flower clusters appear in spring among the leaves; while not overly showy, they attract a wide assortment of insects. After flowering, trees produce dangling clusters of distinctive, round, winged, waferlike fruit, which helps give the species its other common name of Wafer Ash. (The fruits also bear a passing resemblance to hops, explaining its primary common name.) Relatively easy to grow, trees are highly adaptable to various soil and light conditions, and they are drought tolerant once established. Common Hoptree makes a lovely specimen that is ideal for use near a patio, where it adds significant interest to the landscape.

Attracts butterflies, bees, flies, and other pollinators; serves as a larval host for the Giant Swallowtail Butterfly (Heraclides cresphontes); songbirds and small mammals feed on the seeds; provides nesting sites for songbirds.

Eastern Redbud

Scientific Name *Cercis canadensis*

Family Fabaceae

Plant Characteristics Small, deciduous tree up to 30 feet tall; large, green leaves are heart-shaped; small, pealike flowers are rosy pink and grow in clusters on short stalks along the branches.

USDA Hardiness Zones 5a–7b

Bloom Period Early spring–midspring

Growing Conditions Full sun to partial shade and moist, well-drained soils.

Eastern Redbud is a distinctive and highly ornamental tree found across southern portions of the region. One of the first trees to bloom in spring, its bare branches explode with profuse clusters of rich, rosy-pink flowers that brighten up the early-season landscape. This relatively short, often multiple-trunked or low-branching tree makes a wonderful specimen, grouped together or combined with white-flowering dogwoods for a real pop of spring color. Trees have a spreading but often irregular crown packed with large, heart-shaped leaves on somewhat arching branches; they can also be used as understory trees in more-open woodland sites. The mass of spring blooms attracts a multitude of insect pollinators, from butterflies to bees and many more. The blooms provide key forage at a time when other food sources are limited. The flowers give way to elongated and flattened, beanlike pods that turn dark brown at maturity. Easily grown and long-lived, Eastern Redbud benefits from consistent moisture, but the soil must be well drained. Several commercial cultivars are available.

Attracts butterflies, bees, flies, and other pollinators. Larval host for Henry's Elfin Butterfly (Callophrys henrici); *birds eat the seeds.*

159

Florida Dogwood

Scientific Name *Cornus florida*

Family Cornaceae

Plant Characteristics Small, deciduous tree up to 35 feet tall; oval leaves are bright green and prominently veined, often with a somewhat wavy margin; small, rounded clusters of inconspicuous, greenish-yellow flowers are surrounded by 4 large, oval, pure-white bracts.

USDA Hardiness Zones 5a–7b

Bloom Period Spring

Growing Conditions Full sun to partial shade and acidic, sandy, organically rich, average to moist, well-drained soils.

Also called Flowering Dogwood, this lovely native brightens the spring landscape with a profusion of flattened, showy, white blooms—actually white bracts surrounding the inconspicuous central flower cluster—that typically appear before the leaves emerge. While typically a small understory tree of rich woodlands and mixed forests, it has become a popular landscape tree. Highly ornamental, it features low, horizontal, spreading branches that produce a broad, somewhat pyramidal crown from a single trunk or multiple trunks. After flowering, clusters of fleshy, bright-red fruits adorn the branches and later fall to the ground. As fall approaches, the green leaves transition to an attractive reddish maroon. Florida Dogwood is generally easy to grow and makes a wonderful addition to a woodland garden, a good fit for naturalizing, or an attractive specimen plant. It looks particularly showy when combined with other spring-flowering trees such as Eastern Redbud (page 159). Numerous commercial cultivars are available.

Attracts butterflies, bees, and other insect pollinators; serves as a host plant for the Spring Azure Butterfly (Celastrina ladon). Fruits are eaten by songbirds, game birds, and various mammals.

Foxglove Beardtongue

Scientific Name *Penstemon digitalis*

Family Scrophulariaceae

Plant Characteristics Upright, herbaceous perennial up to 5 feet tall; long, elliptical to broad, lance-shaped green leaves have smooth to toothed margins; elongated, branched, terminal clusters of tubular, bell-shaped, white flowers, each with 3 lower lobes and 2 upper lobes.

USDA Hardiness Zones 3a–7b

Bloom Period Early summer–midsummer

Growing Conditions Full sun to partial shade and average to dry, well-drained soils.

This is a lovely wildflower of woodland openings; forest margins; and various open habitats, including old fields, and pastures. Plants thrive in full sun and benefit from regular irrigation. A clump-forming perennial, Foxglove Beardtongue boasts attractive green basal leaves that are often tinged with purple. Typically beginning in early summer, plants produce sturdy, upright, flowering stalks with an abundance of showy, inch-long white blossoms reminiscent of Common Foxglove. Remaining in flower for a month or so, they attract a range of pollinators and add a cheery pop of brightness to the landscape. They are particularly stunning in larger drifts or masses. Plants are tolerant of drought and a wide range of soils, but they benefit from regular moisture and increased soil fertility; they are easily grown from root division or seed. Foxglove Beardtongue works well as part of a perennial border, in a cottage or pollinator garden, and for naturalizing in meadows and fields. A few cultivars are commercially available, including 'Husker Red,' which has attractive purplish leaves.

Attracts butterflies, bees, sphinx moths, and hummingbirds.

Golden Alexanders

Scientific Name *Zizia aurea*

Family Apiaceae

Plant Characteristics Herbaceous perennial 1–3 feet tall; leaves are shiny, dark green, compound, with 3–5 leaflets of variable size and shape with serrated margins; some leaflets may also be lobed; broad, terminal, flat clusters of tiny, yellow flowers.

USDA Hardiness Zones 3a–7b

Bloom Period Late spring–early summer

Growing Conditions Full sun to partial light shade and somewhat average to moist, organically rich, well-drained soils.

This attractive member of the carrot family is a relatively long spring bloomer, adding some needed early-season cheer and interest to the landscape. The plant's broad, airy, golden-yellow flower clusters pop against the contrasting profusion of glossy, dark-green leaves. Like those of dill, fennel, and coriander, the tiny blooms are a magnet for a wide range of smaller pollinators and beneficial insects. Golden Alexanders thrives in bright, moist sites and is a great addition to wet meadows or fields, mesic open woodlands, or rain and butterfly gardens. It is equally useful for a perennial border or even a container planting. Although plants tend to be somewhat short-lived, they readily reseed and often form small, low-growing colonies.

Attracts butterflies, bees, and other insect pollinators; serves as an important native larval host for the Eastern Black Swallowtail (Papilio polyxenes).

Horseflyweed

Scientific Name *Baptisia tinctoria*

Family Fabaceae

Plant Characteristics Bushy, herbaceous perennial up to 3 feet or slightly more in height; compound, gray-green leaves are divided into 3 leaflets that are rounded at the tips; bright-yellow (occasionally lighter yellow), pealike flowers grow in short, somewhat loose, terminal clusters; black, oval, inflated seedpods have pointed tips.

USDA Hardiness Zones 3a–7b

Bloom Period Late spring–early summer

Growing Conditions Performs best in full sun to partial shade and average to dry, well-drained soils.

An underutilized native of dry woodlands and barrens, Horseflyweed forms deep roots and dense, rounded clumps over time. As a result, it is quite durable and long-lived, tolerating drought, fire, and nutrient-poor soils, as well as being largely unpalatable to a range of browsing critters, including deer. Plants boast attractive gray-green foliage and a shrubby, compact form that is often wider than it is tall. Horseflyweed is also known as Yellow Wild Indigo—a reference to its buttery yellow blooms, which typically appear around early summer and are regularly visited by bumblebees. After several weeks of flowering, stubby, inflated seedpods begin to form and eventually turn black when mature, remaining on the plant and providing much visual interest well into winter. The small, loose seeds inside produce a rattling sound when the pods are shaken. Horseflyweed is easily grown and makes a showy addition to a cottage garden or perennial border; it is also good for broader naturalizing in an open woodland or other native setting.

Attracts bees; larval host plant for Frosted Elfin (Callophrys irus) and Wild Indigo Duskywing (Erynnis baptisiae) Butterflies.

169

Marsh Marigold

Scientific Name *Caltha palustris*

Family Ranunculaceae

Plant Characteristics Upright perennial up to 2½ feet tall; rounded, heart-shaped, glossy, green leaves with toothed margins; small, branched clusters of waxy, bright-yellow flowers.

Hardiness Zone 3a–7b

Bloom Period Midspring–early summer

Growing Conditions Full sun to partial shade and moist to wet soils.

A true wetland species, Marsh Marigold boasts a mounding form and handsome, glossy, violetlike leaves. The plant thrives in consistently wet, boggy sites and can even tolerate standing water. It is an attractive addition to rain and water gardens, pond or stream margins, or other low areas of the landscape, where its buttercup-yellow blooms add a bright shot of color. Although not a pollinator magnet, the conspicuous flowers appeal to many bees and flies, providing valuable early-season floral resources. It makes a particularly impressive display when planted en masse. Marsh Marigold is easy to grow; requires little, if any, maintenance; and is virtually pest-free.

Attracts bees and flies; seeds are consumed by many game birds and small mammals; provides cover for wildlife.

Maryland Senna

Scientific Name *Senna marilandica*

Family Fabaceae

Plant Characteristics Upright, herbaceous perennial up to 6 feet in height; long, compound, ferny, green leaves with up to 12 pairs of oblong to elliptical leaflets; terminal and axillary clusters of bright-yellow, pealike flowers.

USDA Hardiness Zones 4a–7b

Bloom Period Summer–early fall

Growing Conditions Full sun to partial shade and average to moist, well-drained soils; adapts well to a variety of garden soils.

With its large, airy, locustlike leaves, this stately perennial adds both stature and a distinctive soft texture to the landscape. Extremely attractive individually or in smaller groups, it is easy to grow, highly adaptable to a variety of well-drained soils, and tolerant of increased summer heat and humidity. Maryland Senna is a pleasing addition to any native garden or meadow, or the back of a perennial border. Beginning in midsummer, plants begin producing showy clusters of golden-yellow flowers that are frequently visited by bumblebees and other native bees. Each leaf petiole possesses an extrafloral nectary, a nectar-producing gland outside the flower at its base that attracts a wide variety of additional beneficial insects, including ants, flies, and wasps. The copious blooms are quickly replaced by elongated, pendulous, beanlike seedpods.

Attracts butterflies, bees, and other insect pollinators; serves as a larval host for Cloudless Sulphur (Phoebis sennae) and Sleepy Orange (Abaeis nicippe) Butterflies, both in southern portions of the region; seeds are fed on by various songbirds and game birds.

New Jersey Tea

Scientific Name *Ceanothus americanus*

Family Rhamnaceae

Plant Characteristics Upright, deciduous shrub up to 3 feet tall or more and just as wide; rough, hairy, oblong leaves have finely toothed margins; small, white flowers grow in dense, rounded clusters.

USDA Hardiness Zones 4a–7b

Bloom Period Spring

Growing Conditions Full sun or partial shade and average to dry, well-drained soils.

This charming branched, deciduous native has a compact and somewhat rounded growth habit. Considered a subshrub, it may die back to the ground in winter, especially when young, but it becomes more woody with age. It thrives in sunny locations with average moisture levels but can adapt to poor soil. The long-lived plants grow slowly and develop a deep root system, making them quite drought tolerant once established. New Jersey Tea is a great addition to any native garden or wildlife garden; in dry, open woodlands; along forest edges; or on rocky slopes. It can be used individually, for naturalizing, or even as a distinctive short hedge. It produces a profusion of delicate, somewhat fuzzy-looking, rounded, pure-white flower heads that are a true favorite of pollinators. Deer, rabbits, and other wildlife often browse on the foliage.

Attracts butterflies, bees, and other insect pollinators, as well as hummingbirds; serves as a larval host for Mottled Duskywing (Erynnis martialis), *Summer Azure* (Celastrina neglecta), *and Spring Azure* (Celastrina ladon) *Butterflies; seeds are fed upon by various songbirds.*

New York Ironweed

Scientific Name *Vernonia noveboracensis*

Family Asteraceae

Plant Characteristics Stout, upright, clump-forming, herbaceous perennial up to 7 feet tall; elongated, lance-shaped, dark-green leaves with serrated margins; dense, somewhat flat, fuzzy-looking, terminal clusters of deep-purple flowers.

USDA Hardiness Zones 5a–7b

Bloom Period Late summer–early fall

Growing Conditions Full sun to partial shade and moist, organically rich, well-drained soils.

New York Ironweed is a tall and robust wildflower found in moist meadows, wet roadside swales, and along wetland borders. Despite its preference for damp sites, it adapts well to fertile garden soils and is a great addition to rain and wildlife gardens or at the back of a perennial border. It can tolerate short periods of drought but will quickly show signs of stress. The statuesque, leafy plants add both texture and structure, being the ideal backdrop or companion for other late-season perennials, including Cutleaf Coneflower (page 229), Dense Blazing Star (page 61), and New England Aster (page 81). The loosely branched clusters of deep-purple, almost neon-looking blooms are stunning and readily entice a wide range of insets to visit. Plants readily self-seed under ideal conditions and are great for naturalizing in larger native spaces.

Attracts butterflies, bees, and other insect pollinators; songbirds readily consume the seeds.

Northern Spicebush

Scientific Name *Lindera benzoin*

Family Lauraceae

Plant Characteristics Deciduous shrub up to 12 feet tall or more; leaves are large, dark green, and elliptical; small axillary clusters of tiny fragrant yellow flowers grow along the brown branches.

USDA Hardiness Zones 4a–7b

Bloom Period Early spring

Growing Conditions Full sun to partial shade and moist, well-drained soils.

This attractive, multistemmed shrub is found in rich, moist woodlands. Plants have a rounded, open growth habit and can be quite ornamental. In early spring, the bare, speckled branches burst forth with a profusion of small, yellow flower clusters, with male and female flowers appearing on different plants. Although not overly showy, the fragrant blooms help brighten the early-spring landscape and attract a variety of insect pollinators. They are quickly replaced by smooth, green leaves that are quite aromatic when crushed, inspiring Northern Spicebush's distinctive name. Later in the season, female plants showcase a bounty of shiny red fruit, often against a backdrop of attractive, bright-yellow fall foliage. The resulting small, oval fruits are readily consumed by hungry songbirds. Plants are relatively easy to grow and quite adaptable to soil and light conditions, but they often do best in light or dappled shade with regular moisture. Northern Spicebush makes an attractive addition to any woodland or rain garden, as well as a distinctive shrubby border.

Attracts butterflies, bees, flies, and other pollinators; a larval host for the Spicebush Swallowtail Butterfly (Papilio troilus).

179

Obedient Plant

Scientific Name *Physostegia virginiana*

Family Lamiaceae

Plant Characteristics Upright, herbaceous perennial up to 4 feet tall (or taller); elongated, lance-shaped, green leaves have toothed margins; dense spikes of tubular, 2-lipped, pink to purple flowers are borne on sturdy, erect stems.

USDA Hardiness Zones 3a–7b

Bloom Period Midsummer–early fall

Growing Conditions Full sun to partial shade and organically rich, average to moist, well-drained soils.

Showy and somewhat underused, Obedient Plant is native to moist meadows, bogs, stream margins, and wetland borders. While it is an excellent addition to these natural landscapes, especially in numbers, it is also easy to grow in rich garden soil with regular irrigation; it does not perform well in poor, dry soils and is relatively intolerant of drought. Mature plants tend to flop a bit and often require staking. Under optimal conditions, it can spread somewhat aggressively by seed or underground rhizomes, and it demands annual maintenance or division to keep in check. A later-season bloomer, it produces impressive spires of large, snapdragon-like flowers that are regularly visited by bees, butterflies, and hummingbirds. Several commercial cultivars are available, including those that are more compact or have white blooms. Obedient Plant is a handsome addition to rain gardens or perennial borders; it is also good for naturalizing along pond margins or in wet meadows. The plant's unique name comes from the fact that individual flowers can be repositioned and remain in place as if they were on hinges.

Attracts butterflies, sphinx moths, bees, and hummingbirds.

Ohio Spiderwort

Scientific Name *Tradescantia ohiensis*

Family Commelinaceae

Plant Characteristics Clump-forming, upright, herbaceous perennial up to 3 feet or slightly more in height and about as wide; long, smooth, grasslike, green leaves wrap around the unbranched green stems; small clusters of dark-blue to violet flowers, each with 3 broad, rounded petals and bright-yellow anthers.

USDA Hardiness Zone 4a–7b

Bloom Period Spring–summer

Growing Conditions Full sun to partial shade and dry to moist, well-drained soils

This low-maintenance and highly distinctive native wildflower is underused as a landscape plant. Ohio Spiderwort's linear, grasslike foliage adds both interest and texture to the landscape. The vibrant blue flowers, with noticeable yellow anthers that appear to almost hover above each blossom, provide an abundance of high-quality pollen for foraging bees. Although Ohio Spiderwort has a relatively long bloom period, individual flowers last but a day at most, typically opening during the morning hours and closing by the afternoon on warm, sunny days. Highly adaptable to a variety of light and soil conditions, it benefits from extra moisture but is tolerant of drought once established. Plants excel in rich soil with consistent moisture and are capable of forming large, rounded clumps. Its overall appearance can become a bit untidy as the summer progresses, so combine it with a variety of attractive companion plants for best results, or cut back to encourage regrowth. Ohio Spiderwort spreads via seed and can become a bit aggressive under ideal conditions; nonetheless, it is a worthy addition to a perennial border, cottage garden, or wildflower meadow.

Attracts western honey bees and many native bees, especially bumblebees.

Partridge Pea

Scientific Name *Chamaecrista fasciculata*

Family Fabaceae

Plant Characteristics Upright to sprawling, herbaceous annual 1–3 feet tall; compound, fernlike, green leaves, each with numerous oblong leaflets; axillary clusters of irregular, butter-yellow flowers with red stamens on reddish-green stems.

USDA Hardiness Zones 3a–7b

Bloom Period Summer–early fall

Growing Conditions Full sun to partial shade and average to dry, well-drained soils.

An early colonizer of open, disturbed sites, Partridge Pea offers tremendous wildlife value, but its beauty as a landscape plant is often underappreciated. This durable annual of southern portions of the region tolerates poor growing conditions, establishes rapidly, and helps fix atmospheric nitrogen into the soil. As a result, it is excellent for naturalizing larger areas and is frequently used to stabilize slopes and prevent erosion. Plants have an airy, fernlike appearance that adds soft texture to the landscape and provides useful cover for wildlife. Individual leaves are somewhat sensitive to touch and tend to close up when disturbed. The showy yellow blooms are particularly attractive to bees. The leaf petioles additionally possess nectar-producing glands (extrafloral nectaries) that attract ants, wasps, and other highly beneficial insects. Plants produce copious amounts of seed and freely self-sow. The resulting seed is an important food source for many songbirds, turkeys, quail, and ducks, as well as small mammals.

Attracts many pollinators; serves as a larval host for Gray Hairstreak (Strymon melinus)*, Cloudless Sulphur* (Phoebis sennae)*, and Little Yellow* (Pyrisitia lisa) *Butterflies.*

185

Pawpaw

Scientific Name *Asimina triloba*

Family Annonaceae

Plant Characteristics Small, deciduous tree up to 30 feet in height; large, oval to oblong, green leaves that droop somewhat downward on branches; nodding, leathery, reddish-brown flowers grow on short stalks from the branches.

USDA Hardiness Zones 5a–7b

Bloom Period Spring

Growing Conditions Full sun to partial shade and fertile, moist, well-drained soils.

This distinctive native understory tree is found in southern and western portions of the region. In the spring, just before (or as) the leaves emerge, the plants produce highly distinctive nodding flowers. The reddish-brown blooms are fleshy in appearance and heavily veined, and they emit a slight odor of rotting carrion. The putrid aroma attracts flies and some beetles, which pollinate the flowers. The flowers are followed by large leaves that are particularly shiny when young. Fertilized flowers develop into large, oblong, and fleshy edible fruit. While not a flashy plant, Pawpaw is easy to grow in moist, rich soils and is a great choice for a wildlife garden or for naturalizing in or near wooded landscapes. As fall approaches, the large, somewhat drooping green leaves turn yellow, making for a handsome autumnal display.

Attracts flies and beetles; serves as a larval host for the Zebra Swallowtail Butterfly (Eurytides marcellus).

Pin Cherry

Scientific Name *Prunus pensylvanica*

Family Rosaceae

Plant Characteristics Deciduous tree up to 35 feet tall; oval to elliptical, shiny, dark-green leaves have finely serrated margins and a pointed tip on reddish-brown branches; terminal, small, somewhat flat clusters of white, 5-petaled flowers have noticeably yellow anthers; bright-red fruit is round, shiny, berrylike.

USDA Hardiness Zones 3a–7b

Bloom Period Late spring–early summer

Growing Conditions Performs best in full sun to partial shade and average to moist, organically rich, well-drained soils.

A native understory tree, Pin Cherry inhabits open woods and clearings, forest margins, and adjacent meadows or disturbed sites. It is fast-growing, provides season-long interest, and offers exceptional wildlife value. Beginning in late spring, trees burst forth with a dramatic show of bright-white flowers just as the glossy green leaves are emerging. The abundant early-season blooms draw in a wide array of flower-visiting insects. As summer proceeds, round, berrylike fruits adorn the branches, turning bright red when ripe. They are readily eaten by various songbirds and small mammals, as well as Black Bears. In autumn, trees become ablaze with orange-red leaves that provide a stunning color show. Even in winter, the shiny, reddish-brown to gray bark with noticeable pale pores (lenticels) lends considerable interest to the landscape.

Attracts many insect pollinators; serves as a larval host for Coral Hairstreak (Satyrium titus)*, Spring Azure* (Celastrina ladon)*, Red-Spotted Purple* (Limenitis arthemis astyanax)*, and Eastern Tiger Swallowtail* (Papilio glaucus) *Butterflies; birds eat the fruit.*

Pink Swamp Milkweed

Scientific Name *Asclepias incarnata*

Family Apocynaceae

Plant Characteristics Upright, clump-forming, herbaceous perennial up to 5 feet in height; narrow, lance-shaped, green leaves; tight, flat clusters of fragrant, light-pink to rose-colored flowers atop branched stems.

USDA Hardiness Zones 3a–7b

Bloom Period Summer–early fall

Growing Conditions Full sun to light shade and moist soils; adaptable to a range of garden soils if regular irrigation is available.

This moisture-loving native is yet another landscape-worthy milkweed. It is common in marshes, wet roadside ditches, and wet meadows throughout the region. A graceful, branched perennial, Pink Swamp Milkweed is an excellent addition to a rain garden, sunny wetland margin, or any wet area of a landscape. It also adds height and interest when incorporated in a container garden. It is widely used by Monarchs as a larval host, but the delicate blooms attract myriad additional insect pollinators. As a result, it is also ideal for naturalizing or incorporating into broader wetland restoration projects. Easy to grow from seed or cuttings, Pink Swamp Milkweed requires little care once established, other than regular moisture. It is one of the most common native milkweed species available commercially. The popular cultivar 'Ice Ballet' has elegant pure-white flowers with somewhat darker green foliage.

Attracts butterflies, bees, and other insect pollinators, as well as hummingbirds; serves as a larval host for the Monarch Butterfly (Danaus plexippus).

Purplestem Angelica

Scientific Name *Angelica atropurpurea*

Family Apiaceae

Plant Characteristics Stout, upright, herbaceous perennial up to 6 feet or more in height; large, compound, dark-green leaves have several toothed, oval leaflets; large, domed clusters of numerous tiny, greenish-white flowers are borne on tall, purplish, hollow stems.

Hardiness Zone 3b–7b

Bloom Period Spring–summer

Growing Conditions Performs best in full sun to light shade and moist to wet, organically rich, well-drained soils.

An impressive plant in form and stature, Purplestem Angelica ranks as one of the tallest wildflowers in the region. Lower portions of the plant are adorned with compound, somewhat ferny-looking leaves that can approach 2 feet in length. As its name suggest, the plant's sturdy, soaring stems are tinged with purple, providing a lovely accent to the darker green foliage. Starting in late spring, plants produce tall stalks that render broad, umbrella-like flower heads many inches across. The tiny whitish flowers attract myriad smaller insect pollinators. A wetland species found in marshes and soggy meadows, along streams, or in wet ditches, Purplestem Angelica thrives in sites with dappled shade and regular moisture, and it can even tolerate regular inundation. It is perfect for naturalistic landscapes or as a specimen in a rain or wildlife garden. It serves as a larval host for the Eastern Black Swallowtail Butterfly (*Papilio polyxenes*).

Attracts butterflies, bees, and other insect pollinators.

Pussy Willow

Scientific Name *Salix discolor*

Family Salicaceae

Plant Characteristics Large, deciduous shrub up to 20 feet tall; stiff, lance-shaped to elliptical, green leaves have slightly toothed margins; compact, silky, gray catkins are produced on bare stems.

Hardiness Zone 2a–7b

Bloom Period Spring

Growing Conditions Full sun to partial shade and moist to wet, well drained soils.

A true harbinger of spring, this familiar shrub is well known for its distinctive and highly ornamental fuzzy catkins that appear on bare branches well before the leaves emerge. It is a dioecious species, meaning male and female flowers are produced on different plants. While both are attractive, the male blooms represent the traditional downy, gray catkins that are most frequently pictured or commonly sold with early-season floral bouquets. They soon begin to open, showcasing an abundance of yellow stamens that offer a great early-season pollen source for bees. Fast-growing, with a strongly upright, rounded growth habit, Pussy Willow boasts leaves that are noticeably silvery underneath, giving plants an overall grayish-green appearance. Best grown in wet areas, it tends to sucker readily from the roots and can form dense stands over time.

Attracts butterflies, bees, and other insect pollinators; serves a larval host for Acadian Hairstreak (Strymon acadica), Mourning Cloak (Nymphalis antiopa), and Viceroy (Limenitis archippus) Butterflies; provides cover and nesting resources for songbirds; buds are eaten by mammals and some game birds.

Red Maple

Scientific Name *Acer rubrum*

Family Sapindaceae

Plant Characteristics Deciduous tree up to 70 feet tall or more, with 3–5 broad, lobed, green leaves with toothed margins on long, red stems; small clusters of tiny, red flowers; pink to reddish, paired, winged fruit that turns light brown when mature.

USDA Hardiness Zones 3a–7b

Bloom Period Early spring

Growing Conditions Full sun to partial shade and moist, well-drained soils.

Aptly named, this attractive native tree sports flashes of red throughout the growing season. Starting in early spring, Red Maple produces clusters of small, reddish flowers that adorn bare branches before the leaves emerge. They are particularly beneficial to bees, offering a plentiful source of nutrient-rich pollen and nectar before many other plants are even in bloom. Hanging, red-tinged, winged seeds and young leaves soon follow. The traditional palm-shaped leaves quickly mature to dark green with lighter green-gray undersides. The real show, though, occurs in autumn, when the foliage bursts into brilliant red. Red Maple is a vigorous grower and quite adaptable in the landscape, being a sound low-maintenance choice. It thrives in moist conditions and can even tolerate temporary inundation. Highly ornamental, it is great for wild spaces or as a specimen or shade tree. Red Maple is a high-wildlife-value tree; birds and squirrels readily consume the seeds. Several commercial cultivars are available.

Attracts bees and birds; serves as a larval host for many showy moth species, including the Io Moth (Automeris io)*, Imperial Moth* (Eacles imperialis)*, Polyphemus Moth* (Antheraea polyphemus)*, and Rosy Maple Moth* (Dryocampa rubicunda)*.*

Scarlet Beebalm

Scientific Name *Monarda didyma*

Family Lamiaceae

Plant Characteristics Upright, clump-forming, herbaceous perennial up to 4 feet tall; aromatic, broadly lance-shaped, dark-green leaves have toothed margins; dense, rounded heads of brilliant red, tubular flowers are borne atop sturdy, square stems.

USDA Hardiness Zones 4a–7b

Bloom Period Midsummer–early fall

Growing Conditions Full sun to partial shade and organically rich, average to moist soils.

Highly ornamental, Scarlet Beebalm is a true stunner when in bloom. As its name suggests, this perennial produces showy but somewhat ragged, rounded clusters of elongated, brilliant red, tubular flowers, with each head measuring up to 4 inches across. It is prolific and blooms for a relatively long period of time, staying productive for many weeks. Regular deadheading encourages more flower production. Like other members of the *Monarda* (beebalm) genus, it is adored by butterflies, hummingbirds, sphinx moths, and larger long-tongued bees. The coarse, dark-green leaves emit a minty odor when handled or crushed. Plants perform best in sunny locations with the right garden soil and consistent moisture, but they can also accommodate some shade. Plants quickly expand in size and spread by both seed and underground rhizomes, forming larger colonies. Scarlet Beebalm is susceptible to powdery mildew, a fungal infection that can occur, particularly during rainy periods or under crowded conditions that limit air circulation. That problem aside, it is a superb accent plant that is useful in perennial borders, cottage gardens, or larger native landscapes. Several commercial cultivars are available.

Particularly attractive to butterflies, sphinx moths, bees, and hummingbirds.

Spotted Beebalm

Scientific Name *Monarda punctata*

Family Lamiaceae

Plant Characteristics Compact, upright, herbaceous
perennial up to 3 feet in height; aromatic, lance-shaped,
green to gray-green leaves have toothed margins;
rounded heads of pale-yellow, tubular flowers are
spotted with purple. Flower heads occur in several tiers
up the sturdy, square stem, directly above a whorl of
colorful, cream to rosy-pink bracts.

USDA Hardiness Zones 3a–7b

Bloom Period Midsummer–early fall

Growing Conditions Full sun to partial shade and dry, well-drained,
sandy soils.

This somewhat obscure native beebalm also goes by the name Dotted
Horsemint. A highly durable plant, it can tolerate both poor soil and
drought but benefits from consistent moisture in garden settings for
the best performance. Ideal for naturalizing in larger landscapes or
in smaller gardens and borders, it is a truly distinctive and somewhat
untamed-looking addition. The dense clusters of small, two-lipped
flowers are overshadowed by the more conspicuous bracts below,
which range in color from cream to rosy pink. The overall effect is
quite showy. With each stem sporting several tiers of blooms, the
overall appearance resembles a pagoda, drawing in a wide range of
insects and, of course, Ruby-Throated Hummingbirds. Plants are
tough and virtually maintenance-free once established, with a relatively long bloom period extending into early autumn. They spread
somewhat quickly by both seed and underground rhizomes, making
Spotted Beebalm ideal for naturalizing in larger, open landscapes.

Attracts butterflies, sphinx moths, bees, wasps, and hummingbirds.

Spotted Geranium

Scientific Name *Geranium maculatum*

Family Geraniaceae

Plant Characteristics Herbaceous perennial up to 2 feet in height; palm-shaped, dark-green leaves with 5 deep lobes, each with a coarsely toothed margin; loose, terminal clusters of open, saucer-shaped flowers, each with 5 rounded, pinkish-purple petals.

Hardiness Zone 3a–7b

Bloom Period Spring–early summer

Growing Conditions Full sun to partial shade and moist, organically rich, well-drained soils.

Spotted Geranium is a common spring wildflower of rich woodlands. This clump-forming perennial features a loose, mounded growth habit and attractive lobed foliage. In late spring, plants begin producing small clusters of cheery, inch-wide, lilac-colored blooms on slender, upright stalks. The floral resources of pollen and nectar attract an array of early-season bees, butterflies, and other flower-visiting insects. Also called Crane's Bill, as fertilized flowers give rise to distinctive elongated, beaked seed capsules that resemble the namesake bird's head. The resulting seeds provide beneficial food for songbirds and small mammals. While plants perform best in light or sun-dappled shade, they can tolerate full sun with consistent moisture and fertile soil. Spotted Geranium is a wonderful addition to a woodland garden, cottage garden, or perennial border. As plants colonize by shallow underground rhizomes, it's also ideal for naturalizing or as an attractive ground cover. A few cultivars are commercially available that offer white flowers or darker leaves.

Attracts butterflies, bees, and many other insect pollinators; birds eat the seeds.

Swamp Rose

Scientific Name *Rosa palustris*

Family Rosaceae

Plant Characteristics Upright, deciduous shrub up to 7 feet tall or more; compound, dark-green leaves on reddish-brown, spiny branches; individual leaflets are oval to elliptical, with serrated margins on spreading branches; broad, 5-petaled, light-pink flowers with yellow centers.

USDA Hardiness Zones 4a–7b

Bloom Period Summer

Growing Conditions Full sun to partial shade and moist to wet, organically rich soils.

As its name suggests, Swamp Rose is a wetland shrub encountered in marshes, swamps, wet meadows, streambanks, and boggy ditches. Plants have a broadly spreading form and are often wider than they are tall; they feature arching, reddish branches with sharp, recurved thorns that require caution when handling. Sizable and attractive rosy-pink flowers are produced during the summer months. The broad blooms offer copious pollen and are visited by a broad range of insects. Later on in the season, plants produce shiny, red hips that remain on the plant after the leaves have fallen, providing additional food for wildlife. The combination of orange-red fall foliage and colorful fruit is quite attractive. Swamp Rose is best grown in perpetually moist sites with acidic soils. The suckering plants can spread and may be somewhat aggressive in smaller spaces. Carolina Rose (*Rosa carolina*) is similar-looking but somewhat more compact and more adapted to drier conditions.

Attracts butterflies, bees, flies, beetles, and other pollinators; fruit is eaten by songbirds, game birds, and small mammals; the densely branched plants provide a cover and nesting resource for songbirds.

Turk's-Cap Lily

Scientific Name *Lilium superbum*

Family Liliaceae

Plant Characteristics Upright, herbaceous perennial up to 6 feet or slightly more in height; smooth, lance-shaped, green leaves in staggered whorls along a central, unbranched, green stem; 1 to many terminal, nodding, yellow-orange to red-orange flowers on long stalks, each flower featuring 6 highly recurved tepals; a purple-spotted throat; and long, protruding anthers.

Hardiness Zone 5a–7b

Bloom Period Early summer–midsummer

Growing Conditions Full sun to partial shade and organically rich, moist, well-drained soils.

Found across southern portions of the region, Turk's-Cap Lily is a beautiful wildflower of wet meadows; wet, deciduous woodland margins and openings; and even boggy roadsides. It superficially resembles Canada Lily (page 143), but it is generally taller, and the showy, pendulous blooms feature tepals that are highly recurved, so much so that the tips generally touch one another. When in flower, it provides a highly ornamental display that is especially eye-catching when planted in groupings. Plants perform best in organically rich soils with regular moisture, and they adapt well to garden settings. They are a glorious addition to perennial borders and rain or water gardens; they can also be used along wetlands or rich woodland margins. The tall plants often benefit from the support of adjacent vegetation; other than this, Turk's-Cap Lily is easy to grow and requires little maintenance once established.

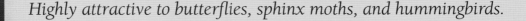

Highly attractive to butterflies, sphinx moths, and hummingbirds.

White Turtlehead

Scientific Name *Chelone glabra*

Family Scrophulariaceae

Plant Characteristics Upright, herbaceous perennial up to 4 feet in height; narrow, lance-shaped, dark-green leaves with serrated margins on sturdy stems; dense, terminal spikes of creamy-white to slightly pinkish, 2-lipped flowers.

USDA Hardiness Zones 3a–7b

Bloom Period Summer–early fall

Growing Conditions Full sun to partial shade and moist to wet, organically rich soils.

This clump-forming wetland species is typically encountered along streams and in wet meadows, fens, and marshes. It thrives in organically rich, moist soils and makes an attractive addition to natural landscapes, as well as a showy accent in rain gardens, butterfly gardens, or perennial borders with regular moisture. While it grows well in sun to partial shade, plants in lower-light environments often get leggy and may require staking; they are also intolerant of dry conditions and drought. White Turtlehead gets its unique name from the distinctive, snapdragon-like flowers, the lower lip of which resembles a turtle's head sticking out of its shell. The dense, cream to pale-pink-infused flower clusters provide a lovely show starting in midsummer and are frequently visited by bumblebees and hummingbirds.

Attracts butterflies, bees, and hummingbirds; serves as a larval host for the Baltimore Checkerspot Butterfly (Euphydryas phaeton).

Wild Bergamot

Scientific Name *Monarda fistulosa*

Family Lamiaceae

Plant Characteristics Upright, herbaceous perennial up to 4 feet tall; aromatic, gray-green, oblong leaves have toothed margins; dense, rounded heads of tubular, light-powdery-pink flowers sit atop green to purplish-green, square stems.

USDA Hardiness Zones 3a–7b

Bloom Period Summer–early fall

Growing Conditions Full sun to partial shade and organically rich, dry to moist, well-drained soils; adapts well to a variety of garden soils and is drought tolerant once established.

Also called beebalm, this widespread, relatively common, colony-forming native is an exceptional plant for pollinators. Butterflies, hummingbirds, and a broad range of other flower visitors adore this plant when it's in bloom. It is a particular favorite of fritillaries and swallowtails. The individual, tubular, powdery-pink-to-lavender flowers form dense, somewhat ragged heads with leafy bracts underneath. Like many other members of the mint family, it boasts square stems and pleasantly aromatic leaves. A prolific bloomer that flowers for a relatively long period of time, Wild Bergamot is tolerant of a wide range of light and soil conditions, including drought and nutrient-poor soil. As a result, it is a great choice for a variety of landscape settings, including everything from herb gardens, perennial borders, and native gardens to larger meadows, open woodlands, and forest margins. Combines well with Common Milkweed (page 49), Black-Eyed Susan (page 41), Garden Phlox (page 69), and other colorful, sun-loving perennials. Like the similar-looking Scarlet Beebalm (page 199), Wild Bergamot is susceptible to powdery mildew. Several commercial cultivars are available.

Attracts butterflies, sphinx moths, bees, and hummingbirds.

211

Wild Lupine

Scientific Name *Lupinus perennis*

Family Fabaceae

Plant Characteristics Upright, clump-forming, herbaceous perennial up to 2 feet in height or slightly more; palmlike, compound, green leaves with up to 11 oblong to elliptical leaflets; leaves occur alternately on branched, reddish stems; elongated, terminal clusters of violet-blue, pealike flowers; elongated, hairy, beanlike seedpods with pointed tips.

USDA Hardiness Zones 3a–7b

Bloom Period Late spring–early summer

Growing Conditions Performs best in full sun to partial shade and average to dry, sandy, well-drained soils.

This is a lovely native wildflower of dry woods, barrens, and savannas, as well as disturbed sites such as power-line cuts and roadsides. Wild Lupine is rare and declining in most states due to loss and fragmentation of habitat; it additionally benefits from regular disturbance, predominantly by prescribed fire or mechanical mowing. Without disturbance, woody plants can quickly encroach and outcompete these plants or decrease open, exposed areas that allow for expanded colonization. In a landscape setting, Wild Lupine adds interest and color to dry garden sites, particularly those with sandy soils; it's also good for naturalizing in meadows or sparse woodlands. The vibrant violet-blue flowers are showy against the darker green backdrop of the palm-shaped leaves and are particularly stunning when planted in larger masses. The blossoms are loved by a variety of native bees.

Attracts bees and butterflies; serves as a larval host for Karner Blue (Lycaeides melissa samuelis), *Frosted Elfin* (Callophrys irus), *Wild Indigo Duskywing* (Erynnis baptisiae), *and Persius Duskywing* (Erynnis persius); *songbirds and small mammals feed on the seeds.*

Wild Sweetwilliam

Scientific Name *Phlox maculata*

Family Polemoniaceae

Plant Characteristics Upright, herbaceous perennial up to 3 feet tall; shiny, lance-shaped, dark-green leaves with smooth or finely toothed margins; large, terminal clusters of fragrant, 5-lobed, tubular flowers in shades of pink, lavender, or occasionally white.

USDA Hardiness Zones 3a–7b

Bloom Period Summer–early fall

Growing Conditions Full sun to light shade and average to moist, organically rich, well-drained soils.

Wild Sweetwilliam is a widespread but seldom overly common wildflower of rich woodlands, forest and stream margins, and adjacent open areas across much of the eastern United States. The compact, clump-forming plants spread to form larger colonies under ideal conditions. Thriving in sunny sites with rich, moist soils, they adapt readily to most garden soils, provided there is sufficient organic material and regular irrigation. Plants are also intolerant of drought and, like other phlox species, can be plagued by powdery mildew if adequate plant spacing and air circulation are not provided. The real show starts in summer, when plants produce numerous elongated, scepter-shaped clusters of cheery, pinkish to purplish blooms on distinctive purple-spotted stems. (This trait is the source of one of Wild Sweetwilliam's other common names, Speckled Phlox.) The sweetly scented flowers are a massive draw for many pollinators, from butterflies to hummingbirds, and are a welcome addition to any cottage, perennial, or butterfly garden. Grouping plants together helps maximize the display.

Attracts butterflies, sphinx moths, and hummingbirds.

Woodland Sunflower

Jewelweed

Partial Shade to Full Shade

White Snakeroot

Black Baneberry

Common Blue Violet

Smallspike False Nettle

Bigleaf Aster

Common Pricklyash

From Black Baneberry (page 221) to Jewelweed (page 237), some good wildlife-attracting plants prefer or can tolerate lower light levels. These plants often perform best with 3–6 hours of direct sunlight per day or less. In many cases, they benefit from some sun in the morning or evening, when light intensity is reduced, but they are sensitive to too much sun—which can lead to increased stress, dehydration, even scorching. These plants are often best used along forest margins, under larger trees, in woodland gardens, or in north-facing border gardens.

Virginia Bluebells

Red Columbine

217

Bigleaf Aster

Scientific Name *Eurybia macrophylla*

Family Asteraceae

Plant Characteristics Upright, herbaceous perennial up to 2 feet in height; large, heart-shaped, bright-green leaves with toothed margins; flat, terminal, branched clusters of daisylike, white to light-lavender-colored flowers with bright-yellow centers.

USDA Hardiness Zones 3a–7b

Bloom Period Late summer–fall

Growing Conditions Partial shade to full shade and average to moist, organically rich, well-drained soils.

A lovely wildflower common to woodlands and forest borders, Bigleaf Aster is a reliable choice for more-dimly lit parts of the landscape, thriving best in dappled sunlight. While plants grow well in full shade, flower production is often limited. The species' namesake large, heart-shaped leaves are quite distinctive and become progressively smaller up the stem. They provide a wonderful backdrop to highlight the somewhat sparse yet colorful, branching flower clusters. A wide variety of butterflies, bees, wasps, and other late-season pollinators flock to the blooms. Plants spread readily by underground rhizomes to form larger, dense colonies and can make a highly attractive, shade-loving ground cover. Bigleaf Aster is ideal for naturalizing or to help brighten up darker corners of the garden. Game birds often feed on the seed.

Attracts butterflies, bees, and other insect pollinators.

Black Baneberry

Scientific Name *Actaea racemosa*

Family Ranunculaceae

Plant Characteristics Upright perennial up to 7 feet tall; coarse, compound, green leaves have lobed, oblong leaflets with serrated margins; branched, slender, and elongated clusters of tiny, fuzzy-looking, white flowers.

USDA Hardiness Zones 3a–7b

Bloom Period Early summer–midsummer

Growing Conditions Partial to full shade and moist, organically rich, well-drained soils.

Black Baneberry is large wildflower of moist deciduous forests. It boasts large, compound leaves and a broad, somewhat airy form that can reach 4 feet or more in width. Needless to say, adequate garden space is required to accommodate this impressive plant. In early summer, narrow, elongated clusters of white flowers bloom on minimally branched, towering stalks. The resulting display is quite eye-catching, adding a lovely vertical element and bright pop to woodland gardens, forested stream margins, or the back of a shady perennial border. Also called Black Cohosh, it is easy to grow and adaptable to rich garden soils in partial or full shade; flowering is maximized within light shade. Plants spread by both underground rhizomes and seed. The ornamental cultivar 'Atropurpurea' boasts showy, deep-purple leaves and flower stalks.

Attracts butterflies, bees, and other insect pollinators, as well as hummingbirds; serves as larval host for the Appalachian Azure Butterfly (Celastrina neglectamajor).

Canada Anemone

Scientific Name *Anemone canadensis*

Family Ranunculaceae

Plant Characteristics Upright perennial up to 2 feet in height; palmlike, green leaves with deeply divided primary lobes are further subdivided into secondary toothed lobes; upward-facing flowers with 5 rounded, pure-white petals and yellow anthers are borne on slender, hairy stalks.

USDA Hardiness Zones 2a–7b

Bloom Period Late spring–early summer

Growing Conditions Partial shade to full shade and moist, well-drained soils.

Canada Anemone is a delicate early-season wildflower of wet meadows, moist woodlands, stream banks, and river margins. The cheerful white buttercup-like flowers are borne on slender stems above the rich, green foliage below. While not overly attractive to pollinators, the copious pollen available is appealing to many small native bees and flies. Plants spread by underground rhizomes and can rapidly form large colonies if given the space to expand. Consequently, Canada Anemone is ideal for naturalizing or for use as a showy native ground cover, but it can often overwhelm smaller garden spaces. Tall Thimbleweed (*Anemone virginiana*) is a similar-looking but nonaggressive, garden-worthy alternative. As its name suggests, spent flower heads become elongated, resembling a sewing thimble, before bursting open to release dark, wind-dispersed seeds with fluffy, silky tails.

Attracts small, short-tongued native bees and syrphid (flower) flies.

Common Blue Violet

Scientific Name *Viola sororia*

Family Violaceae

Plant Characteristics Herbaceous perennial up to 8 inches in height; broad, heart-shaped, glossy, green leaves with toothed margins; violet-blue flowers with 5 rounded petals each.

USDA Hardiness Zones 3a–7b

Bloom Period Spring

Growing Conditions Partial shade to full shade and moist, organically rich, well-drained soil.

This cheery and diminutive species—the state flower of Rhode Island and New Jersey—is a common wildflower of woodlands, moist slopes, and creek margins. While it prefers light to partial shade, Common Blue Violet is often encountered in sunny, wet meadows; prairies; and even shaded lawns in more-suburban locations. Exceptionally easy to grow and flexible when used in the landscape, it makes an excellent addition to any wooded garden or rain garden; it also works well in containers on a patio or as a showy ground cover in poorly lit areas of the landscape. Plants freely self-seed, can spread quickly, and can even become a bit weedy. Individual flowers have five flaring, violet-blue petals that are heavily striated at the white throat and are displayed above the broad, green leaves on slender stalks. Both leaves and flowers of this stemless perennial arise from rhizomes at ground level. While primarily spring-blooming, flowers may periodically be produced throughout the growing season.

Attracts butterflies, bees, and other insect pollinators; serves as a larval host for butterflies including the Aphrodite Fritillary (Speyeria aphrodite) and Great Spangled Fritillary (Speyeria cybele).

Common Pricklyash

Scientific Name *Zanthoxylum americanum*

Family Rutaceae

Plant Characteristics Deciduous shrub up to 20 feet in height or more; compound leaves with 5–11 lance-shaped to oblong, green leaflets on distinctive thorny green petioles and gray-brown branches; axillary clusters of small, greenish-yellow flowers.

USDA Hardiness Zones 3a–7b

Bloom Period Spring

Growing Conditions Partial shade to full shade; average to moist, well-drained soils; adapts to a variety of soils; drought tolerant once established.

Also called Northern Pricklyash, this is a fairly widespread shrub that features attractive gray bark and a somewhat irregular, branching habit. Plants are generally multistemmed but may have a single trunk and otherwise resemble a small tree. The ashlike, dark-green leaves are highly aromatic when crushed and also (along with the bark and twigs) numb the mouth if chewed, resulting in the plant's other common name, Toothache Tree. Common Pricklyash's most noteworthy attribute, however, is the prevalence of numerous sharp thorns that cover the plant, requiring caution when handling or maneuvering nearby. A dioecious species, the plant has axillary flower clusters that bloom in spring along the branches; while small and often easy to miss, they are quite attractive to many native bees and flies. The flowers are soon replaced by small, round, berrylike, reddish fruit. Plants spread by underground rhizomes and can form dense thickets over time.

Attracts butterflies, bees, and other insect pollinators; serves as a larval host for the Giant Swallowtail Butterfly (Heraclides cresphontes); birds eat the fruit.

Cutleaf Coneflower

Scientific Name *Rudbeckia laciniata*

Family Asteraceae

Plant Characteristics: Herbaceous perennial up to 8 feet tall; long, smooth, light-green basal leaves have 3–7 deep, toothed lobes with toothed margins; stem leaves may or may not be lobed and become smaller up the plant; large, terminal, daisylike flowers have somewhat drooping, bright-yellow rays and greenish centers atop stiff, slender, branching stems.

Hardiness Zone 3a–7b

Bloom Period Midsummer–early fall

Growing Conditions Partial shade to full shade and moist, organically rich, well-drained soils.

Typically encountered in wet meadows and along moist forest margins and streams, this native moisture-loving perennial is intolerant of dry soils and drought. It nonetheless adapts well to organically rich garden soils with regular irrigation, and it often performs best in partially shaded sites. Forming sizable clumps, it can spread quickly by underground rhizomes and may be somewhat aggressive. This growth habit makes Cutleaf Coneflower ideal for naturalizing or mass-planting. In smaller garden spaces, it is best used at the back of a border, where larger clumps can periodically be divided to help control spread. The showy, bright-yellow flowers are borne on sturdy, upright stems beginning in mid-to-late summer and continue blooming through early fall; they are highly attractive to a wide range of flower-visiting insects. Spent flowers should be regularly deadheaded to encourage reblooming.

Attracts butterflies, bees, and many other insect pollinators; songbirds consume the seeds.

Eastern Waterleaf

Scientific Name *Hydrophyllum virginianum*

Family Boraginaceae

Plant Characteristics: Herbaceous perennial up to 2 feet in height; broad, triangular, compound, green leaves with leaflets or lobes having toothed margins; leaves may be spotted with white; terminal, rounded clusters of lobed, bell-shaped, white to lavender-colored flowers.

Hardiness Zone 4a–7b

Bloom Period Late spring–early summer

Growing Conditions Partial shade to full shade and average to moist, organically rich, well-drained soils.

Also called Virginia Waterleaf, this is a lovely wildflower of rich, deciduous woodlands; forest trails and clearings; and shaded stream margins. The delicate-looking plants have a mounding growth habitat and can spread somewhat aggressively by underground rhizomes to quickly form extensive colonies. While this quality may overwhelm smaller garden spaces, it is ideal for naturalizing, helping with erosion control, or adding an attractive ground cover to more-shaded landscapes. Its highly dissected, often white-spotted leaves provide both interest and soft texture. Later in spring, plants produce small clusters of light-colored, somewhat frilly-looking, bell-shaped flowers that readily attract native bees. Eastern Waterleaf is easily grown in fertile garden soils with some shade. Combine it with other early-season woodland wildflowers, including Common Blue Violet (page 225), Red Columbine (page 241), Spotted Geranium (page 203), and Wild Blue Phlox (page 255) for a handsome effect.

Attracts a variety of native bees, including bumblebees, bee flies, and syrphid (flower) flies.

Feathery False Lily of the Valley

Scientific Name *Maianthemum racemosum*

Family Liliaceae

Plant Characteristics: Upright, unbranched, herbaceous perennial up to 2½ feet in height; large, smooth, broad, oval, green leaves with smooth margins on light-green, somewhat zigzagging stems; terminal, branched, and somewhat fuzzy-looking clusters of small, star-shaped, white flowers.

Hardiness Zone 3a–7b

Bloom Period Late spring–early summer

Growing Conditions Partial shade to full shade and organically rich, average to moist, well-drained soils.

This is a lovely wildflower of rich, deciduous woodlands. Also called False Solomon's Seal, its arching stems and large, handsome, green leaves closely resemble those of *Polygonatum* spp. (true Solomon's Seals). It thrives in partial shade and fertile soil with regular moisture, although it can accommodate somewhat drier conditions and poor soils. An early-season bloomer, the plant produces fuzzy, white, plumelike flower clusters that are reminiscent of Astilbe; though not overly showy, they attract a surprising assortment of small, flower-visiting insects. The flowers are replaced by shiny, red, berrylike fruits that provide food for wildlife. Feathery False Lily of the Valley is probably best used in woodland gardens, lightly shaded borders, or in darker spots to brighten the landscape. Plants slowly expand over time to form larger colonies.

Attracts beetles, bees, and flies; fruit is consumed by songbirds, game birds, and small mammals; foliage provides cover for wildlife.

Hairy Pagoda-Plant

Scientific Name *Blephilia hirsuta*

Family Lamiaceae

Plant Characteristics: Upright perennial up to 3 feet tall; aromatic, oval, light-green to green leaves have toothed margins; whorled, dense axillary clusters of tubular, purple-spotted, white flowers occur spaced out along the hairy, square stems.

Hardiness Zone 4a–7b

Bloom Period Summer

Growing Conditions Partial shade to full shade and organically rich, moist, well-drained soils.

Aptly named, this attractive native features mint-scented foliage and somewhat compact, shaggy-looking flower clusters along the upper, typically unbranched stems that superficially resemble an ornate Japanese pagoda. The two-lipped blooms are popular with a wide range of different insects, particularly long-tongued bees. Also called Hairy Wood Mint, the plant thrives in moist woodlands and associated borders and openings; it is therefore ideal for darker, more shaded locations in the garden. A colony-forming wildflower, Hairy Pagoda-Plant spreads by underground rhizomes and is therefore superb for naturalizing. It is closely related and quite similar in appearance to beebalm (genus *Monarda*); unfortunately, it also shares that plant group's susceptibility to powdery mildew, a common fungal disease that causes whitish-gray patches on leaves and other plant parts. Providing adequate plant spacing and air circulation, as well as avoiding overhead irrigation, can help prevent outbreaks.

Attracts butterflies, bees, wasps, flies, and sphinx moths.

Jewelweed

Scientific Name *Impatiens capensis*

Family Balsaminaceae

Plant Characteristics Upright, herbaceous annual up to 5 feet tall; oval to elliptical, dull-green to bluish-green leaves with coarsely toothed margins and long petioles are borne on smooth, succulent stems; axillary clusters of 1–3, rear-spurred, orange-colored, conically shaped flowers, each with 2 large lower lips and a single upper one, are marked with reddish-brown spots; each flower dangles from a delicate stalk.

USDA Hardiness Zones 2a–7b

Bloom Period Summer–fall

Growing Conditions Partial shade to full shade and organically rich, moist to wet soils.

Jewelweed is a common and distinct annual wildflower of moist woodlands; river, stream, and shaded forest-trail margins; wetlands; and other boggy sites. Its succulent stems are reminiscent of cultivated impatiens and contain a viscous sap that can help relieve the itch and irritation of poison ivy and other rashes. The bushy plants showcase 1-inch-long, pendulous, distinctively cornucopia-shaped orange flowers. After flowering, the plants produce pointed, cylindrical seed capsules that split open explosively when ripe to forcibly disperse the seeds. This somewhat startling action can often be triggered by contact and is the inspiration behind the species' other common name of Touch-Me-Not. It also makes Jewelweed a very effective colonist, capable of forming extensive colonies that return year after year. It is ideal for naturalizing in rich, shade-dappled woodland settings; along wetlands; or in rain gardens.

Attracts butterflies, bees, and hummingbirds; game birds and small mammals often eat the seeds.

Purple Milkweed

Scientific Name *Asclepias purpurascens*

Family Apocynaceae

Plant Characteristics Upright, herbaceous perennial up to 3 feet in height; large, oblong, dark-green leaves with a central purplish vein and often undulating margins; showy, domed clusters of fragrant, deep-pink to reddish-purple flowers.

USDA Hardiness Zones 4a–7b

Bloom Period Summer

Growing Conditions Partial shade to full shade and average to moist, well-drained soils.

With its large clusters of deep rose-colored flowers, this milkweed is a showstopper. The ample blooms are a magnet for butterflies, bees, sphinx moths, and other insect pollinators, as well as hummingbirds. Although similar in appearance and stature to Common Milkweed, Purple Milkweed is not nearly as aggressive; nonetheless, it does still spread by underground rhizomes and can form larger colonies over time, making it less desirable for smaller garden spaces. While Purple Milkweed prefers richer, moist soils and often grows best in a bit of light or dappled shade, it is highly adaptable and can perform well in full sun as well as tolerate short-term drought once established. This species' ornamental nature makes it a great addition to any native or wildlife garden; it's also good for naturalizing in meadows or along woodland borders. After flowering, the plants produce smooth, narrow, and upward-pointing seedpods that eventually burst open to release the silk-laden seeds for wind dispersal.

Very attractive to butterflies, bees, and other insect pollinators, as well as hummingbirds.

Red Columbine

Scientific Name *Aquilegia canadensis*

Family Ranunculaceae

Plant Characteristics Upright, sparsely branched, herbaceous perennial up to 3 feet in height; green leaves are hairy and compound, with each leaflet having rounded lobes; nodding, red-and-yellow, bell-shaped flowers have 5 long spurs.

USDA Hardiness Zones 3a–7b

Bloom Period Spring–early summer

Growing Conditions Partial shade to full shade and average to moist, well-drained soils.

This lovely native woodland wildflower adds beauty and texture to any spring landscape. The compact plant boasts delicate, ferny foliage and distinctive red, pendulous flowers with yellow centers; the flowers are supported on upright, branched stalks. Each flower has five long, curved nectar spurs. Red Columbine is easy to grow and highly adaptable to a variety of well-drained garden soils and light conditions, from full sun to full shade. It benefits from regular moisture if grown in sunnier locations. It readily reseeds and can readily expand in coverage under ideal conditions. The early-blooming flowers are a favorite of hummingbirds and many bees at a time when forage resources are often limited. It is an excellent choice for woodland, shade, and cottage gardens, especially when combined with other colorful spring species such as Wild Blue Phlox (page 255). It is equally ideal for naturalizing.

Attracts butterflies, bees, hummingbirds, and sphinx moths; songbirds consume the seeds; serves as a larval host plant for the Columbine Duskywing Butterfly (Erynnis lucilius).

Smallspike False Nettle

Scientific Name *Boehmeria cylindrica*

Family Urticaceae

Plant Characteristics Upright, herbaceous perennial 1–3 feet tall; broad, prominently veined, dark-green leaves with toothed margins are borne on occasionally branched, green stems; short spikes of small greenish flowers arise from leaf axils.

USDA Hardiness Zones 3b–7b

Bloom Period Summer

Growing Conditions Partial shade to full shade and average to moist, organically rich, well-drained soils.

While not grown for its beauty, this moisture-loving native is a valuable addition to damp woodlands; stream, pond, or other wetland margins; or rain or butterfly gardens with lower light levels. Its preference for shadier locations provides gardeners with added flexibility in the landscape. Aptly named, Smallspike False Nettle closely resembles Stinging Nettle, but it lacks the unpleasant stinging hairs and is thus perfectly safe to handle. Plants are dioecious, with the diminutive flowers being easy to overlook and wind pollinated. Although Smallspike False Nettle is a somewhat scraggly grower, plants can be easily shaped by occasional pruning to keep them more compact and bushy. Plants spread by rhizomes and can be somewhat aggressive in the landscape, especially in smaller spaces.

*Serves as a larval host for Red Admiral (*Vanessa atalanta*), Question Mark (*Polygonia interrogationis*), and Eastern Comma (*Polygonia comma*) Butterflies.*

Smooth Solomon's Seal

Scientific Name *Polygonatum biflorum*

Family Rosaceae

Plant Characteristics: Upright, herbaceous perennial up to 3½ feet in height; oblong to somewhat elliptical, conspicuously veined, green leaves grow on sturdy, arching, and unbranched stems; small, dangling clusters of tubular, bell-shaped, cream flowers are produced from the leaf axils.

Hardiness Zone 3b–7b

Bloom Period Late spring–early summer

Growing Conditions Partial shade to full shade and average to wet, organically rich, well drained soils.

Also called Small Solomon's Seal, this woodland wildflower adds both interest and texture to the landscape. Its graceful, arching stems are adorned with broad, glossy, alternating leaves that have noticeably parallel veins. Starting in late spring, pendulous clusters of creamy-white blooms, reminiscent of small bells, hang below. They are primarily pollinated by native bees but may also periodically attract the odd Ruby-Throated Hummingbird. The showy flowers are replaced by round, bluish-black berries at maturity; these are readily consumed by birds. Plants spread by underground rhizomes to form larger colonies. Smooth Solomon's Seal is low-maintenance and fairly adaptable to a range of light conditions, provided it is grown in rich soil. The glossy, green leaves turn golden yellow in autumn, adding color to the late-season landscape.

Attracts bees; birds eat the fruit.

Sweetscented Joe Pye Weed

Scientific Name *Eutrochium purpureum*

Family Asteraceae

Plant Characteristics: Upright, herbaceous perennial up to 7 feet tall; highly textured, lance-shaped, green leaves with toothed margins occur in whorls spaced out along a sturdy, green stem; fuzzy, mauve-colored flowers occur in large, terminal, rounded clusters.

Hardiness Zone 4a–7b

Bloom Period Midsummer–early fall

Growing Conditions Partial shade to full shade and moist, organically rich, and well-drained soils.

This is a robust and stately wildflower of open woodlands and forest borders. Unlike many pollinator favorites, Sweetscented Joe Pye Weed can perform well across the full spectrum of illumination from full sun to considerable shade, making it a highly flexible landscape addition. The towering plants thrive in moist, organically rich soils and expand into sizable multistemmed clumps over time. Very similar in appearance to Spotted Joe Pye Weed (page 103), it tends to have more-rounded flower clusters and increased height, and it is generally found in sites that are somewhat less wet. The domed, terminal clusters of fragrant, vanilla-scented, mauve flowers are virtually irresistible to butterflies, moths, and bees. Established plants are equally striking individually or en masse, providing a wonderful combination of height, texture, and color. Also called Purple Node Joe Pye Weed, Sweetscented Joe Pye Weed is equally useful used individually at the back of a perennial border, massed together in a larger meadow, or for naturalizing along a moist forest or wetland border.

Attracts butterflies, bees, and many other insect pollinators.

Virginia Bluebells

Scientific Name *Mertensia virginica*

Family Boraginaceae

Plant Characteristics Upright, herbaceous perennial up to 2 feet in height; large, gray-green, oval leaves with prominent veins; terminal clusters of trumpet-shaped, pendulous, tubular, light-blue flowers.

USDA Hardiness Zones 3a–7b

Bloom Period Spring

Growing Conditions Partial shade to full shade and moist, organically rich, well-drained soils.

This is a lovely spring wildflower of moist woodlands and stream or creek margins, often blooming before most trees have fully leafed out. It thrives in moist, fertile soils and grows best in shadier sites in the landscape. A clump-forming perennial, Virginia Bluebells can often form sizable colonies over time under optimal growing conditions. The large, light-colored leaves have a soft, floppy appearance and help brighten the early-season understory landscape; they also provide an excellent backdrop for the showy, trumpet-shaped flowers. Each bud starts out pinkish before soon transforming into the characteristic light-electric-blue color at maturity. The dangling flower clusters, which indeed resemble miniature bells, are regularly visited by bees, butterflies, and sphinx moths. Plants have a relatively long bloom period before dying back to the ground by midsummer. Virginia Bluebells provides early-season interest and color to any moist woodland garden or shadier perennial border. It is additionally an exceptional species for naturalizing.

Attracts butterflies, bees, birds, and other insect pollinators.

Virginia Snakeroot

Scientific Name *Aristolochia serpentaria*

Family Aristolochiaceae

Plant Characteristics: Herbaceous perennial; ranges from 6 inches to 2 feet in height; green, heart-shaped to narrow, spear-shaped leaves on a thin, zigzagging stem; small, purplish-brown, pipe-shaped flowers near the base of the plant.

Hardiness Zone 5a–7b

Bloom Period Late spring–early summer

Growing Conditions Partial shade to full shade and rich, moist, well-drained soils.

This diminutive perennial is widespread in rich woodlands and shady forest edges across southern portions of the region, although you may have to look closely to find it. Plants have an ascending growth habit and a distinctive thin, zigzagging stem. As with other members of the genus *Aristolochia*, the leaves are somewhat heart-shaped but vary greatly in width, from very narrow to more broad. The distinctive pipe-shaped flowers occur low near the ground and often bloom below the leaf litter; they are pollinated by flies and gnats. Plants spread via rhizomes and form small colonies along the forest floor. Virginia Snakeroot is an ideal and highly underutilized species for woodland gardens or other rich, shaded areas in the landscape. A much larger relative, Pipevine (*Aristolochia macrophylla*) is a twining perennial vine with characteristically heart-shaped leaves. It can be grown up trees or on trellises, fences, or arbors.

Attracts flies; larval host for the Pipevine Swallowtail Butterfly (Battus philenor), whose larvae require multiple plants to complete development.

White Snakeroot

Scientific Name *Ageratina altissima*

Family Asteraceae

Plant Characteristics Upright, herbaceous perennial up to 3 feet tall; coarse, lance-shaped to somewhat heart-shaped, dark-green leaves have serrated margins and prominent venation; flat, terminal clusters of small, 5-lobed, fuzzy-looking white flowers are borne on smooth stems.

USDA Hardiness Zones 3a–7b

Bloom Period Late summer–fall

Growing Conditions Partial shade to full shade and organically rich, moist, well-drained soils. It is highly adaptable to a wide range of soil types and conditions.

White Snakeroot is a wildflower of deciduous woodlands, forest margins, and adjacent semiopen areas. Although it thrives in partially shaded sites with fertile, moist soils, plants are quite adaptable and tolerant of drier conditions and even full sun if regular irrigation is provided. It can even be grown in deep shade, but flowering may be limited. As summer nears an end, the somewhat ragged-looking plants explode into bloom, helping to brighten the late-season woodland garden or various dark corners of the landscape. The brilliant snow-white flowers appeal to a broad range of insects, including many small, night-flying moths, which can easily locate the abundant floral resources in low light. Plants remain in bloom for an extended period well into autumn. White Snakeroot can quickly form larger colonies, spreading by a combination of seed and shallow, underground rhizomes. Its alternate common name—Fall Poison—serves as a warning that all parts of the plant are acutely toxic and may be fatal if ingested.

Attracts butterflies, bees, wasps, flies, and moths.

Wild Blue Phlox

Scientific Name *Phlox divaricata*

Family Polemoniaceae

Plant Characteristics Herbaceous, mounding perennial up to 1½ feet in height; elliptical to lance-shaped, green leaves on green, sticky stems; loose, somewhat flat clusters of delicately fragrant, tubular, lilac to light-blue flowers, each with 5 spreading lobes.

USDA Hardiness Zones 3a–7b

Bloom Period Spring

Growing Conditions Partial shade to full shade and organically rich, moist, well-drained soils.

This cheery early-season wildflower of open woodlands, streambanks, forest margins, and adjacent open areas is also called Woodland Phlox. An excellent ground cover, the low-growing clumps spread vegetatively by procumbent stems that root at the node, slowly forming extensive colonies. In spring, the foliage is crowned by loose clusters of showy, pinkish-lavender or icy-blue flowers. The delicate blooms provide a good source of spring nectar for butterflies, hummingbirds, sphinx moths, and many other pollinating insects. The resulting display is particularly attractive en masse. Wild Blue Phlox makes a fine addition to shade, rock, or cottage gardens; open woodlands; perennial borders; or otherwise darker sites in the landscape. Plants are easy to grow but can be susceptible to powdery mildew in sites with poor air circulation and excess moisture. Several cultivars are commercially available.

Attracts butterflies, bees, sphinx moths, and hummingbirds.

Woodland Sunflower

Scientific Name *Helianthus divaricatus*

Family Asteraceae

Plant Characteristics: Upright, herbaceous perennial 3–6 feet in height or slightly more; lance-shaped, yellow-green leaves taper to a short point, occurring as opposite pairs on stiff, green to reddish-brown stems; large, terminal, daisylike flower heads have elongated, bright-yellow petals surrounding a golden center.

Hardiness Zone 3a–7b

Bloom Period Midsummer–early fall

Growing Conditions Partial shade to full shade and average to dry, well-drained soils.

This is a widespread wildflower of drier, open woodlands; forest clearings; and forest borders. The stiff, slender stems boast rough, yellow-green leaves, adding both height and texture to the landscape. Starting around July, the statuesque plants begin producing numerous showy, golden-yellow flowers that help brighten shadier sites. Plants spread vigorously by underground rhizomes and can expand into sizable colonies over time, making this species useful for naturalizing; its aggressive nature can quickly overwhelm smaller garden spaces, however. Woodland Sunflower is easy to grow and quite adaptable to a variety of conditions, requiring little maintenance once established. Paleleaf Woodland Sunflower (*Helianthus strumosus*) is a similar-looking and equally landscape-worthy species.

Attracts butterflies, bees, and other insect pollinators; serves as a larval host for the Silvery Checkerspot Butterfly (Chlosyne nycteis); songbirds, game birds, and various small mammals feed on the seeds.

Zigzag Goldenrod

Scientific Name *Solidago flexicaulis*

Family Asteraceae

Plant Characteristics Upright, typically unbranched, herbaceous perennial up to 3 feet in height; broadly oval, dark-green leaves with toothed margins on a stiff, somewhat zigzagged, green stem; terminal and axillary clusters of small, golden-yellow flowers.

USDA Hardiness Zones 3a–7b

Bloom Period Late summer–fall

Growing Conditions Partial shade to full shade and average to moist, organically rich, well-drained soils.

This is a highly distinctive goldenrod of fertile, deciduous woodlands; trail edges; and stream and woodland margins. It is named for characteristic angled stems that zigzag somewhat between each broad, heavily toothed, dark-green leaf. Blooming well through fall, the sparse, compact, golden flower clusters brighten the late-season forested landscape and provide plentiful resources for foraging insects at a time when many other wildflowers are waning. Thriving in moist conditions in partial or even full shade, Zigzag Goldenrod is easy to grow and well worth the effort. Plants spread slowly by underground rhizomes to form small expanding colonies; as a result, it is particularly useful for naturalizing, but note that it can eventually overtake smaller garden spaces.

Attracts butterflies, bees, flies, beetles, and other pollinators. The seeds are eaten by songbirds and game birds.

Garden Plants for Butterflies

1 **Black-Eyed Susan** (*Rudbeckia hirta*), pg. 41

2 **Blue Vervain** (*Verbena hastata*), pg. 45

3 **Culver's Root** (*Veronicastrum virginicum*), pg. 57

4 **Dense Blazing Star** (*Liatris spicata*), pg. 61

5 **Garden Phlox** (*Phlox paniculata*), pg. 69

6 **Golden Alexanders** (*Zizia aurea*), pg. 165

7 **Lanceleaf Coreopsis** (*Coreopsis lanceolata*), pg. 75

8 **Little Bluestem** (*Schizachyrium scoparium*), pg. 77

9 **Maryland Senna** (*Senna marilandica*), pg. 173

10 **New York Ironweed** (*Vernonia noveboracensis*), pg. 177

11 **Obedient Plant** (*Physostegia virginiana*), pg. 181

12 **Pink Swamp Milkweed** (*Asclepias incarnata*), pg. 191

13 **Purple Coneflower** (*Echinacea purpurea*), pg. 91

14 **Scarlet Beebalm** (*Monarda didyma*), pg. 199

15 **Showy Goldenrod** (*Solidago speciosa*), pg. 97

16 **Sweetscented Joe Pye Weed** (*Eutrochium purpureum*), pg. 247

17 **Turk's-Cap Lily** (*Lilium superbum*), pg. 207

18 **Virginia Mountainmint** (*Pycnanthemum virginianum*), pg. 113

19 **Wild Bergamot** (*Monarda fistulosa*), pg. 211

Garden Plants for Bees

1 **Bluebell Bellflower** (*Campanula rotundifolia*), pg. 135

2 **Blue Mistflower** (*Conoclinium coelestinum*), pg. 131

3 **Blue Wild Indigo** (*Baptisia australis*), pg. 133

4 **Brown-Eyed Susan** (*Rudbeckia triloba*), pg. 137

5 **Butterflyweed** (*Asclepias tuberosa*), pg. 47

6 **Common Milkweed** (*Asclepias syriaca*), pg. 49

7 **Common Sneezeweed** (*Helenium autumnale*), pg. 53

8 **Common Yarrow** (*Achillea millefolium*), pg. 55

9 **Cutleaf Coneflower** (*Rudbeckia laciniata*), pg. 229

10 **Devil's Bite** (*Liatris scariosa*), pg. 63

11 **False Aster** (*Boltonia asteroides*), pg. 65

12 **Foxglove Beardtongue** (*Penstemon digitalis*), pg. 163

13 **Meadowsweet** (*Spiraea alba*), pg. 79

14 **New England Aster** (*Symphyotrichum novae-angliae*), pg. 81

15 **Nodding Onion** (*Allium cernuum*), pg. 83

16 **Ohio Spiderwort** (*Tradescantia ohiensis*), pg. 183

17 **Showy Tick Trefoil** (*Desmodium canadense*), pg. 99

18 **Spotted Beebalm** (*Monarda punctata*), pg. 201

19 **Stiff Goldenrod** (*Oligoneuron rigidum*), pg. 105

20 **Virginia Mountainmint** (*Pycnanthemum virginianum*), pg. 113

Container Garden for Pollinators

1 **Black-Eyed Susan** (*Rudbeckia hirta*), pg. 41

2 **Dense Blazing Star** (*Liatris spicata*), pg. 61

3 **Lanceleaf Coreopsis** (*Coreopsis lanceolata*), pg. 75

4 **Pink Swamp Milkweed** (*Asclepias incarnata*), pg. 191

5 **Purple Coneflower** (*Echinacea purpurea*), pg. 91

3

4

5

Bird Food & Nesting Plants

FULL SUN

COMMON NAME	SCIENTIFIC NAME
Big Bluestem pg. 39	Andropogon gerardii
Black-Eyed Susan pg. 41	Rudbeckia hirta
Common Ninebark pg. 51	Physocarpus opulifolius
Cup Plant pg. 59	Silphium perfoliatum
Devil's Bite pg. 63	Liatris scariosa
Field Thistle pg. 67	Cirsium discolor
Lanceleaf Coreopsis pg. 75	Coreopsis lanceolata
Little Bluestem pg. 77	Schizachyrium scoparium
Meadowsweet pg. 79	Spiraea alba
New England Aster pg. 81	Symphyotrichum novae-angliae
Purple Coneflower pg. 91	Echinacea purpurea
Roughleaf Dogwood pg. 95	Cornus drummondii
Trumpet Honeysuckle pg. 111	Lonicera sempervirens

PARTIAL SHADE TO FULL SHADE

COMMON NAME	SCIENTIFIC NAME
Common Pricklyash pg. 227	Zanthoxylum americanum
Cutleaf Coneflower pg. 229	Rudbeckia laciniata
Feathery False Lily of the Valley, pg. 233	Maianthemum racemosum
Jewelweed pg. 237	Impatiens capensis
Woodland Sunflower pg. 257	Helianthus divaricatus
Zigzag Goldenrod pg. 259	Solidago flexicaulis

FULL SUN TO PARTIAL SHADE

COMMON NAME	SCIENTIFIC NAME
Allegheny Serviceberry pg. 123	Amelanchier laevis
Alternateleaf Dogwood pg. 125	Cornus alternifolia
American Black Elderberry, pg. 127	Sambucus nigra ssp. canadensis
Black Cherry pg. 129	Prunus serotina
Buttonbush pg. 141	Cephalanthus occidentalis
Canada Milkvetch pg. 145	Astragalus canadensis
Chokecherry pg. 149	Prunus virginiana
Common Evening Primrose, pg. 153	Oenothera biennis
Common Hackberry pg. 155	Celtis occidentalis
Common Hoptree pg. 157	Ptelea trifoliata
Florida Dogwood pg. 161	Cornus florida
Marsh Marigold pg. 171	Caltha palustris
Maryland Senna pg. 173	Senna marilandica
New Jersey Tea pg. 175	Ceanothus americanus
New York Ironweed pg. 177	Vernonia noveboracensis
Northern Spicebush pg. 179	Lindera benzoin
Partridge Pea pg. 185	Chamaecrista fasciculata
Pin Cherry pg. 189	Prunus pensylvanica
Pussy Willow pg. 195	Salix discolor
Swamp Rose pg. 205	Rosa palustris
Wild Lupine pg. 213	Lupinus perennis

Hummingbird Plants

FULL SUN

COMMON NAME	SCIENTIFIC NAME
Common Milkweed pg. 49	Asclepias syriaca
Dense Blazing Star pg. 61	Liatris spicata
Devil's Bite pg. 63	Liatris scariosa
Field Thistle pg. 67	Cirsium discolor
Garden Phlox pg. 69	Phlox paniculata
Hoary Vervain pg. 73	Verbena stricta
Ohio Buckeye pg. 85	Aesculus glabra
Swamp Rosemallow pg. 107	Hibiscus moscheutos
Trumpet Honeysuckle pg. 111	Lonicera sempervirens

PARTIAL SHADE TO FULL SHADE

COMMON NAME	SCIENTIFIC NAME
Black Baneberry pg. 221	Actaea racemosa
Jewelweed pg. 237	Impatiens capensis
Purple Milkweed pg. 239	Asclepias purpurascens
Red Columbine pg. 241	Aquilegia canadensis
Wild Blue Phlox pg. 255	Phlox divaricata

FULL SUN TO PARTIAL SHADE

COMMON NAME	SCIENTIFIC NAME
Blue Wild Indigo pg. 133	Baptisia australis
Buttonbush pg. 141	Cephalanthus occidentalis
Canada Lily pg. 143	Lilium canadense
Canada Milkvetch pg. 145	Astragalus canadensis
Cardinal Flower pg. 147	Lobelia cardinalis
Foxglove Beardtongue pg. 163	Penstemon digitalis
Great Blue Lobelia pg. 167	Lobelia siphilitica
New Jersey Tea pg. 175	Ceanothus americanus
Obedient Plant pg. 181	Physostegia virginiana
Pink Swamp Milkweed pg. 191	Asclepias incarnata
Scarlet Beebalm pg. 199	Monarda didyma
Spotted Beebalm pg. 201	Monarda punctata
Turk's-Cap Lily pg. 207	Lilium superbum
White Turtlehead pg. 209	Chelone glabra
Wild Bergamot pg. 211	Monarda fistulosa
Wild Sweetwilliam pg. 215	Phlox maculata

Larval Host List (By Butterfly Species)

If you want to attract caterpillars to your yard, these are the plants to seek out. The following plants are known larval hosts for butterflies. As a bonus, we've included photos of the caterpillars (when possible) and adults to help you get started on identifying any caterpillars you may find.

Red-Spotted Purple
Allegheny Serviceberry, pg. 123
Amelanchier laevis

Spring Azure
Alternateleaf Dogwood pg. 125
Cornus alternifolia
Florida Dogwood, pg. 161
Cornus florida
Roughleaf Dogwood, pg. 95
Cornus drummondii

Arogos Skipper
Cobweb Skipper
Common Wood Nymph
Dusted Skipper
Big Bluestem, pg. 39
Andropogon gerardii

Appalachian Azure
Black Baneberry, pg. 221
Actaea racemosa

Coral Hairstreak
Eastern Tiger Swallowtail
Red-Spotted Purple
Summer Azure
Black Cherry, pg. 129
Prunus serotina

Silvery Checkerspot
Black-Eyed Susan, pg. 41
Rudbeckia hirta
Woodland Sunflower, pg. 257
Helianthus divaricatus

Wild Indigo Duskywing
Blue Wild Indigo, pg. 133
Baptisia australis

Cherry Gall Azure
Coral Hairstreak
Red-Spotted Purple
Chokecherry, pg. 149
Prunus virginiana

Aphrodite Fritillary
Great Spangled Fritillary
Meadow Fritillary
Variegated Fritillary
Common Blue Violet, pg. 225
Viola sororia

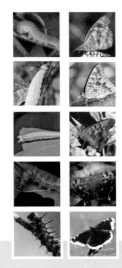

American Snout
Hackberry Emperor
Tawny Emperor
Question Mark
Mourning Cloak

Common Hackberry, pg. 155
Celtis occidentalis

Giant Swallowtail

Common Hoptree, pg. 157
Ptelea trifoliata
Common Pricklyash, pg. 227
Zanthoxylum americanum

Monarch

Common Milkweed, pg. 49
Asclepias syriaca

Pink Swamp Milkweed, pg. 191
Asclepias incarnata

Purple Milkweed, pg. 239
Asclepias purpurascens

Whorled Milkweed, pg. 117
Asclepias verticillata

Painted Lady

Field Thistle, pg. 67
Cirsium discolor

Black Swallowtail

Golden Alexanders, pg. 165
Zizia aurea
Purplestem Angelica, pg. 193
Angelica atropurpurea

Northern Cloudywing
Silver-Spotted Skipper
Question Mark

Hairy Lespedeza, pg. 71
Lespedeza hirta

Frosted Elfin
Wild Indigo Duskywing

Horseflyweed, pg. 169
Baptisia tinctoria

Cobweb Skipper
Common Wood Nymph
Crossline Skipper
Dusted Skipper
Indian Skipper
Leonard's Skipper
Swarthy Skipper

Little Bluestem, pg. 77
Schizachyrium scoparium

Cloudless Sulphur
Sleepy Orange

Maryland Senna, pg. 173
Senna marilandica

Northern Azure
Spring Azure

Meadowsweet, pg. 79
Spiraea alba

Mottled Duskywing
Spring Azure
Summer Azure

New Jersey Tea, pg. 175
Ceanothus americanus

Spicebush Swallowtail

Northern Spicebush, pg. 179
Lindera benzoin

Cloudless Sulphur
Little Yellow
Gray Hairstreak

Partridge Pea, pg. 185
Chamaecrista fasciculata

Zebra Swallowtail

Pawpaw, pg. 187
Asimina triloba

Coral Hairstreak
Eastern Tiger Swallowtail
Red-Spotted Purple
Spring Azure

Pin Cherry, pg. 189
Prunus pensylvanica

Acadian Hairstreak
Question Mark
Viceroy

Pussy Willow, pg. 195
Salix discolor

Eastern Tailed-Blue
Frosted Elfin
Gray Hairstreak
Northern Cloudywing
Southern Cloudywing

Showy Tick Trefoil, pg. 99
Desmodium canadense

Question Mark
Red Admiral

Smallspike False Nettle, pg. 243
Boehmeria cylindrica

Pearl Crescent

Smooth Blue Aster, pg. 101
Symphyotrichum laeve

Pipevine Swallowtail

Virginia Snakeroot, pg. 251
Aristolochia serpentaria

American Lady
Painted Lady

Western Pearly Everlasting,
pg. 115
Anaphalis margaritacea

Baltimore Checkerspot

White Turtlehead, pg. 209
Chelone glabra

Karner Blue
(federally endangered)

Persius Duskywing
Wild Indigo Duskywing

Wild Lupine, pg. 213
Lupinus perennis

271

RETAIL SOURCES OF NORTHEAST NATIVE SEED & PLANTS

Audubon Native Plants Database
www.audubon.org/native-plants
(512) 232-0100
(*Searchable database returns links to local retail suppliers.*)

Ernst Seeds
www.ernstseed.com
8884 Mercer Pike
Meadville, PA 16335
(800) 873-3321

Grow Native Massachusetts
www.grownativemass.org/great-resources
/nurseries-seed

The Native Plant Trust
(*formerly the New England Wildflower Society*)
www.nativeplanttrust.org
180 Hemenway Road
Framingham, MA 01701
(508) 877-7630

New England Wetland Plants, Inc.
www.newp.com/catalog/seed-mixes
14 Pearl Lane
South Hadley, MA 01075
(413) 548-8000

Prairie Moon Nursery
www.prairiemoon.com
32115 Prairie Lane
Winona, MN 55987
(866) 417-8156

Prairie Nursery
www.prairienursery.com
P.O. Box 306
Westfield, WI 53964
(800) 476-9453

The Xerces Society for Invertebrate Conservation
www.xerces.org/pollinator-conservation
/pollinator-friendly-plant-lists

COOPERATIVE EXTENSION SERVICE

Nearly every county in the U.S. has an extension office, where experts from state universities provide scientific knowledge and expertise to the public on various topics, including natural resources, agriculture, and horticulture. They are often excellent resources for gardeners and those planning a native garden. The **National Pesticide Information Center** maintains an interactive directory of extension offices across the country: npic.orst.edu/pest/countyext.htm.

NATIVE PLANT SOCIETIES

The **American Horticultural Society** provides an online directory of native plant societies in the U.S. and Canada: www.ahsgardening.org/gardening-resources/societies-clubs-organizations/native -plant-societies.

BOTANICAL GARDENS & ARBORETUMS

The **American Horticultural Society** also maintains an interactive directory of U.S. botanical gardens and arboretums, which is searchable by zip code: www.ahsgardening.org/gardening-programs /rap/the-garden-guide.

Index

A

Acer rubrum, 30–31, 197
Achillea millefolium, 24–25, 55
Actaea racemosa, 32–33, 221
Aesculus glabra, 26–27, 85
Ageratina altissima, 34–35, 253
Allegheny Serviceberry, 28–29, 123
Allium cernuum, 26–27, 83
Alternateleaf Dogwood, 28–29, 125
Amelanchier laevis, 28–29, 123
American Black Elderberry, 28–29, 127
American Elder, 127
American Wahoo, 139
Anaphalis margaritacea, 26–27, 115
Andropogon gerardii, 24–25, 39
Anemone canadenis, 32–33, 223
Anemone virginiana, 32–33, 223
Angelica atropurpurea, 30–31, 193
Aquilegia canadensis, 32–33, 241
Aristolochia macrophylla, 251
Aristolochia serpentaria, 34–35, 251
Arnoglossum atriplicifolium, 26–27, 87
Asclepias incarnata, 30–31, 191
Asclepias purpurascens, 32–33, 239
Asclepias syriaca, 24–25, 49
Asclepias tuberosa, 24–25, 47
Asclepias verticillata, 26–27, 117
Asimina triloba, 30–31, 187
Astragalus canadenis, 28–29, 145

B

Baptisia australis, 28–29, 133
Baptisia tinctoria, 30–31, 169
Big Bluestem, 24–25, 39
Bigleaf Aster, 32–33, 219
Black Baneberry, 32–33, 221
Black Cherry, 28–29, 129
Black Cohosh, 221
Black-Eyed Susan, 24–25, 41
Blephilia hirsuta, 32–33, 235
Bluebell Bellflower, 28–29, 135
Blue Flag Iris, 24–25, 43
Blue Mistflower, 28–29, 131
Blue Vervain, 45
Blue Wild Indigo, 28–29, 133
Boehmeria cylindrica, 32–33, 243
Boltonia asteroides, 24–25, 65
Brown-Eyed Susan, 28–29, 137
Burningbush, 28–29, 139
Butterflyweed, 24–25, 47
Buttonbush, 28–29, 141

C

Caltha palustris, 30–31, 171
Campanula rotundifolia, 28–29, 135
Canada Anemone, 32–33, 223
Canada Lily, 28–29, 143
Canada Milkvetch, 28–29, 145
Cardinal Flower, 28–29, 147
Carolina Rose, 205
Ceanothus americanus, 30–31, 175
Celtis occidentalis, 28–29, 155
Cephalanthus occidentalis, 28–29, 141
Cercis canadensis, 28–29, 159
Chamaecrista fasciculata, 30–31, 185
Chelone glabra, 32–33, 209
Chokecherry, 28–29, 149
Cirsium discolor, 24–25, 67
Common Blue Violet, 32–33, 225
Common Boneset, 28–29, 151
Common Elderberry, 127
Common Evening Primrose, 28–29, 153
Common Hackberry, 28–29, 155
Common Hoptree, 28–29, 157
Common Milkweed, 24–25, 49
Common Ninebark, 24–25, 51
Common Pricklyash, 32–33, 227
Common Sneezeweed, 24–25, 53
Common Yarrow, 24–25, 55
Conoclinium coelestinum, 28–29, 131
Coral Honeysuckle, 111
Coreopsis lanceolata, 24–25, 75
Cornus alternifolia, 28–29, 125
Cornus drummondii, 26–27, 95
Cornus florida, 28–29, 161
Cornus racemosa, 95
Crane's Bill, 203
Crimsoneyed Rosemallow, 107
Culver's Root, 24–25, 57
Cup Plant, 24–25, 59
Cutleaf Coneflower, 32–33, 229

D

Dense Blazing Star, 24–25, 61
Desmodium canadense, 26–27, 99
Devil's Bite, 24–25, 63
Dotted Horsemint, 201
Drymocallis arguta, 26–27, 109

E

Eastern Redbud, 28–29, 159
Eastern Waterleaf, 32–33, 231
Echinacea purpurea, 26–27, 91
Euonymus atropurpureus, 28–29, 139
Eupatorium perfoliatum, 28–29, 151
Eurybia macrophylla, 32–33, 219
Eutrochium maculatum, 26–27, 103
Eutrochium purpureum, 34–35, 247

F

Fall Poison, 253
False Aster, 24–25, 65
False Solomon's Seal, 32–33, 233
Feathery False Lily of the Valley, 32–33, 233
Field Thistle, 24–25, 67
Filipendula rubra, 26–27, 93
Florida Dogwood, 28–29, 161
Flowering Dogwood, 161
Foxglove Beardtongue, 30–31, 163

G

Garden Phlox, 24–25, 69
Geranium maculatum, 30–31, 203
Golden Alexanders, 30–31, 165
Gray Dogwood, 95
Great Blue Lobelia, 30–31, 167

H

Hairy Lespedeza, 24–25, 71
Hairy Pagoda-Plant, 32–33, 235
Hairy Wood Mint, 235
Hardy Ageratum, 131
Harebell, 28–29, 135
Helenium autumnale, 24–25, 53
Helianthus divaricatus, 34–35, 257
Helianthus strumosus, 257
Hibiscus moscheutos, 26–27, 107
Hoary Vervain, 24–25, 73
Horseflyweed, 30–31, 169
Hydrophyllum virginianum, 32–33, 231

I

Impatiens capensis, 32–33, 237
Iris virginica, 24–25, 43

J

Jewelweed, 32–33, 237

L

Lanceleaf Coreopsis, 24–25, 75
Lespedeza hirta, 24–25, 71
Liatris scariosa, 24–25, 63
Liatris spicata, 24–25, 61
Lilium canadense, 28–29, 143
Lilium superbum, 32–33, 207
Lindera benzoin, 30–31, 179
Little Bluestem, 24–25, 77
Lobelia cardinalis, 28–29, 147
Lobelia siphilitica, 30–31, 167
Lonicera sempervirens, 26–27, 111
Lupinus perennis, 32–33, 213
Lythrum alatum, 26–27, 119

M

Maianthemum racemosum, 32–33, 233
Marsh Blazing Star, 61
Marsh Marigold, 30–31, 171
Maryland Senna, 30–31, 173
Meadowsweet, 26–27, 79

Mertensia virginica, 34–35, 249
Monarda didyma, 30–31, 199
Monarda fistulosa, 32–33, 211
Monarda punctata, 30–31, 201

N

New England Aster, 26–27, 81
New Jersey Tea, 30–31, 175
New York Ironweed, 30–31, 177
Nodding Onion, 26–27, 83
Northern Pricklyash, 32–33, 227
Northern Spicebush, 30–31, 179

O

Obedient Plant, 30–31, 181
Oenothera biennis, 28–29, 153
Ohio Buckeye, 26–27, 85
Ohio Spiderwort, 30–31, 183
Oligoneuron rigidum, 26–27, 105

P

Pagoda Dogwood, 125
Pale Indian Plantain, 26–27, 87
Paleleaf Woodland Sunflower, 257
Partridge Pea, 30–31, 185
Pasture Thistle, 67
Pawpaw, 30–31, 187
Penstemon digitalis, 30–31, 163
Phlox divaricata, 34–35, 255
Phlox maculata, 32–33, 215
Phlox paniculata, 24–25, 69
Physocarpus opulifolius, 24–25, 51
Physostegia virginiana, 30–31, 181
Pickerelweed, 26–27, 89
Pin Cherry, 30–31, 189
Pink Swamp Milkweed, 30–31, 191
Pipevine, 251
Polygonatum biflorum, 32–33, 245
Pontederia cordata, 26–27, 89
Prairie Cinquefoil, 109
Prunus pensylvanica, 30–31, 189
Prunus serotina, 28–29, 129
Prunus virginiana, 28–29, 149
Ptelea trifoliata, 28–29, 157
Purple Coneflower, 26–27, 91
Purple Milkweed, 32–33, 239
Purple Node Joe Pye Weed, 247
Purplestem Angelica, 30–31, 193
Pussy Willow, 30–31, 195
Pycnanthemum virginianum, 26–27, 113

Q

Queen of the Prairie, 26–27, 93

R

Red Columbine, 32–33, 241
Red Maple, 30–31, 197
Rosa carolina, 205
Rosa palustris, 32–33, 205

Roughleaf Dogwood, 26–27, 95
Rudbeckia hirta, 24–25, 41
Rudbeckia laciniata, 32–33, 229
Rudbeckia triloba, 28–29, 137

S
Salix discolor, 30–31, 195
Sambucus nigra ssp. *canadensis,* 28–29, 127
Scarlet Beebalm, 30–31, 199
Schizachyrium scoparium, 24–25, 77
Senna marilandica, 30–31, 173
Showy Goldenrod, 26–27, 97
Showy Tick Trefoil, 26–27, 99
Silphium perfoliatum, 24–25, 59
Small Solomon's Seal, 245
Smallspike False Nettle, 32–33, 243
Smooth Blue Aster, 26–27, 101
Smooth Solomon's Seal, 32–33, 245
Solidago flexicaulis, 34–35, 259
Solidago speciosa, 26–27, 97
Speckled Phlox, 215
Spiraea alba, 26–27, 79
Spotted Beebalm, 30–31, 201
Spotted Geranium, 30–31, 203
Spotted Joe Pye Weed, 26–27, 103
Stiff Goldenrod, 26–27, 105
Summer Phlox, 69
Swamp Rose, 32–33, 205
Swamp Rosemallow, 26–27, 107
Sweetscented Joe Pye Weed, 34–35, 247
Symphyotrichum laeve, 26–27, 101
Symphyotrichum novae-angliae, 26–27, 81

T
Tall Cinquefoil, 26–27, 109
Tall Thimbleweed, 223
Toothache Tree, 227
Touch-Me-Not, 237
Tradescantia ohiensis, 30–31, 183
Trumpet Honeysuckle, 26–27, 111
Turk's-Cap Lily, 32–33, 207

V
Verbena hastata, 24–25, 45
Verbena stricta, 24–25, 73
Vernonia noveboracensis, 30–31, 177
Veronicastrum virginicum, 24–25, 57
Viola sororia, 32–33, 225
Virginia Bluebells, 34–35, 249
Virginia Iris, 43
Virginia Mountainmint, 26–27, 113
Virginia Snakeroot, 34–35, 251
Virginia Waterleaf, 231

W
Wafer Ash, 157
Western Pearly Everlasting, 26–27, 115
White Snakeroot, 34–35, 253
White Turtlehead, 32–33, 209

Whorled Milkweed, 26–27, 117
Wild Bergamot, 32–33, 211
Wild Blue Phlox, 34–35, 255
Wild Lupine, 32–33, 213
Wild Sweetwilliam, 32–33, 215
Winged Loosestrife, 119
Winged Lythrum, 26–27, 119
Woodland Phlox, 255
Woodland Sunflower, 34–35, 257

Y
Yellow Wild Indigo, 169

Z
Zanthoxylum americanum, 32–33, 227
Zigzag Goldenrod, 34–35, 259
Zizia aurea, 30–31, 165

Notes

Notes

Photo Credits

Interior photos by Jaret C. Daniels except as noted below. All photos copyright of their respective photographers.
Aaron Carlson: 104, 119, 201; **sonnia hill:** 70

These images are licensed under the CC0 1.0 Universal (CC0 1.0) Public Domain Dedication license, which is available at https://creativecommons.org/publicdomain/zero/1.0/ or licensed under Public Domain Mark 1.0, which is available at https://creativecommons.org/publicdomain/mark/1.0/: **ALAN SCHMIERER:** 271 (Persius Duskywing butterfly); **Andy Wilson:** 177; **caryaovata:** 109; **Chrissy McClarren and Andy Reago:** 270 (Mottled Duskywing butterfly); **Craig Martin:** 168; **Dave Miller:** 115; **De Tuin:** 98; **Haneesh K M.:** 269 (Indian Skipper larva); **Jason Swanson:** 259; **khteWisconsin:** 270 (Acadian Hairstreak butterfly); **Lynn Harper:** 189; **Miranda Kohout:** 238; **Nathan Rauh:** 139; **NC Wetlands:** 242; **peakaytea:** 209; **Robb Hannawacker:** 117; **Stephanie Coutant:** 258; **Todd Eiben:** 270 (Southern Cloudywing butterfly); **US Forest Service, Superior National Forest, by Steve Robertsen:** 219

These images are licensed under the Attribution 2.0 Generic (CC BY 2.0) license, which is available at https://creativecommons.org/licenses/by/2.0/: **Andrew Cannizzaro:** 38, no modifications, original image at https://www.flickr.com/photos/acryptozoo/21321111812/, 62, no modifications, original image at https://www.flickr.com/photos/acryptozoo/21304763556/; **Andrey Zharkikh:** 108, no modifications, original image at https://www.flickr.com/photos/zharkikh/50142761551/; **benet2006:** 235, no modifications, original image at https://www.flickr.com/photos/benetd/14524273888/; **Bob Peterson:** 21 (bottom 6), no modifications, original image at https://www.flickr.com/photos/pondapple/6245406089/, 185, no modifications, original image at https://www.flickr.com/photos/pondapple/5761053027/; **Doug McGrady:** 79, no modifications, original image at https://www.flickr.com/photos/douglas_mcgrady/41890536140, 142, no modifications, original image at https://www.flickr.com/photos/douglas_mcgrady/35936024802/, 176, no modifications, original image at https://www.flickr.com/photos/douglas_mcgrady/36601496635/; **jimduggan24:** 118, no modifications, original image at https://www.flickr.com/photos/126765045@N07/49643244937/; **Judy Gallagher:** 268 (Silvery Checkerspot larva), no modifications, original image at https://www.flickr.com/photos/52450054@N04/36002798142/, 268 (Wild Indigo Duskywing butterfly), no modifications, original image at https://www.flickr.com/photos/52450054@N04/20647547121/; **LEONARDO DASILVA:** 96, no modifications, original image at https://www.flickr.com/photos/leonardodasilva/32122871718/; 97, no modifications, original image at https://www.flickr.com/photos/leonardodasilva/44086650335/; **Lydia Fravel:** 66, no modifications, original image at https://www.flickr.com/photos/158105449@N02/51413611576/; **Michele Dorsey Walfred:** 124, no modifications, original image at https://www.flickr.com/photos/dorseymw/47727763952/; **NC Wetlands:** 205, no modifications, original image at https://www.flickr.com/photos/ncwetlands/35494662680/; **Sam Fraser-Smith:** 173, no modifications, original image at https://www.flickr.com/photos/samfrasersmith/3728562352/; **schizoform:** 187, no modifications, original image at https://www.flickr.com/photos/schizoform/51139661389/; **Under the same moon...:** 208, no modifications, original image at https://www.flickr.com/photos/71119007@N03/48649062712/

These images are licensed under the Attribution 4.0 International (CC BY 4.0) license, which is available at https://creativecommons.org/licenses/by/4.0/: **Andrew Meeds:** 269 (Northern Cloudywing larva), no modifications, original image at https://www.inaturalist.org/photos/30731691; **Andrew Sebastian:** 149, no modifications, original image at https://www.inaturalist.org/photos/146441630; **Andy Deans:** 268 (Appalachian Azure larva), no modifications, original image at https://www.inaturalist.org/photos/137727389; **Blake Bringhurst:** 95, no modifications, original image at https://www.inaturalist.org/photos/150794412; **Bonnie Semmling:** 250, no modifications, original image at https://www.inaturalist.org/photos/91688337; **botanygirl:** 107, no modifications, original image at http://www.inaturalist.org/photos/509595, 143, no modifications, original image at https://www.inaturalist.org/photos/28588229, 245, no modifications, original image at http://www.inaturalist.org/photos/591360; **Chris McAnlis:** 233, no modifications, original image at https://www.inaturalist.org/photos/75011969; **christine123:** 270 (Northern Azure larva), no modifications, original image at https://www.inaturalist.org/photos/12561505; **Colin Croft:** 268 (Great Spangled Fritillary larva), no modifications, original image at https://www.inaturalist.org/photos/41280746; **Daniel S. Katz:** 87, no modifications, original image at https://www.inaturalist.org/photos/147931322; **David Weisenbeck:** 101, no modifications, original image at https://www.inaturalist.org/photos/94848534; **dvollmar:** 268 (Arogos Skipper butterfly), no modifications, original image at https://www.inaturalist.org/photos/100866992; **Elias:** 63, no modifications, original image at https://www.inaturalist.org/photos/156814426; **Elliot Greiner:** 71, no modifications, original image at https://www.inaturalist.org/photos/154597812; **erothsch:** 268 (Appalachian Azure butterfly), no modifications, original image at https://www.inaturalist.org/photos/128526145; **Even Dankowicz:** 99, no modifications, original image at https://www.inaturalist.org/photos/123720834; **Isaac Krone:** 145, no modifications, original image at http://www.inaturalist.org/photos/4528913; **Jason Ksepka:** 251, no modifications, original image at https://www.inaturalist.org/photos/135180956; **Katja Schulz:** 197, no modifications, original image at https://www.inaturalist.org/photos/57159297; **Lillie:** 77, no modifications, original image at https://www.inaturalist.org/photos/168849527; **Matt Berger:** 116, no modifications, original image at https://www.inaturalist.org/photos/153781583; **Mathew Zappa:** 138, no modifications, original image at https://www.inaturalist.org/photos/19621129, 234, no modifications, original image at https://www.inaturalist.org/photos/86992085; **Mobjackbayboy:** 106, no modifications, original image at https://www.inaturalist.org/photos/93991342; **Patrick Hanly:** 193, no modifications, original image at https://www.inaturalist.org/photos/139812716; **Nick Block:** 268 (Cherry Gall Azure Butterfly), no modifications, original image at http://www.inaturalist.org/photos/2701860; **Peter Chen 2.0:** 246, no modifications, original image at https://www.inaturalist.org/photos/66306097; **Sam Kieschnick:** 269 (Hackberry Emperor larva), no modifications, original image at https://www.inaturalist.org/photos/24777615; **threelark:** 231, no modifications, original image at https://www.inaturalist.org/photos/77129247

About the Author

Jaret C. Daniels, PhD, is a curator at the Florida Museum of Natural History's McGuire Center for Lepidoptera and Biodiversity and a professor of entomology at the University of Florida, specializing in insect ecology and conservation. He is also a professional nature photographer, author, and native plant enthusiast. He has written numerous scientific papers, popular articles, and books on wildflowers, wildlife landscaping, insects, and butterflies, including butterfly field guides for Florida, Georgia, the Carolinas, Ohio, and Michigan. His other books for Adventure Publications include *Native Plant Gardening for Birds, Bees & Butterflies: South; Native Plant Gardening for Birds, Bees & Butterflies: Southeast; Native Plant Gardening for Birds, Bees & Butterflies: Upper Midwest; Backyard Bugs: An Identification Guide to Common Insects, Spiders, and More;* and *Insects & Bugs for Kids: An Introduction to Entomology.* Jaret lives in Gainesville, Florida, with his wife, Stephanie.